CAPITALISM: A CRIME STORY

"In this enthralling and eminently readable book, Harry Glasbeek explains how liberal law strives to reconcile capitalism with liberalism. Thanks to law's burnishing, capitalism acquires a liberal-hued patina of legitimacy. However, beneath the surface, cherished liberal principles are contorted or simply sacrificed for the sake of capitalism's ideological needs. In clear and powerful prose, Glasbeek offers us a piercing lens and a transformed language through which to see and to condemn capitalist power. This book is essential reading for those who wish to understand the world in order to change it."

> — Julian Sempill, senior lecturer, Faculty of Law, University of
> Melbourne and author of *Power and the Law*

"*Capitalism: A Crime Story* contests the stories about law told by a wide gamut of capitalist fanatics, from corporate law professionals to legal academics—apologists who incredulously avert their eyes from the deceptive and deviant conduct of corporate capital. Glasbeek illustrates how law's tangled web shrouds the corporate form, masking the ways corporate capitalist coercion receives privileged treatment under law. Not satisfied to merely pierce the corporate veil, Glasbeek annihilates apologist narratives by rebuking the entrenched techniques of corporate profiteering and refuting the notion that capitalist business behaviour is distinct from the notion of a crime. Corporate capitalist wrongdoing is no mere aberration, it is the norm."

> — Adrian A. Smith, Department of Law & Legal Studies,
> Carleton University

"Harry Glasbeek has done it again: another eloquent and accessible book for non-lawyers and lawyers alike, exposing capitalism's betrayal of basic liberal values and law's role as an accessory. From the Westray disaster to the devastation at Lac Mégantic, he shows how the lawlessness of corporations stands in sharp contrast to our expectations that individuals be both free of coercion and responsible for the harms caused by their actions. At this critical juncture we face the imminent loss of a habitable planet, yet Glasbeek shows a way forward to confronting the inherent criminality of capitalism."

— Elizabeth Sheehy, professor of law, University of Ottawa

"Glasbeek eloquently demonstrates that the theory and application of corporate law is antithetical to our norms and values of individual liberty and autonomy. By exposing the unequal power relationships prevailing under contemporary capitalism he challenges others to view the law as it is, and not as it has been sold to us."

— Peter Grabosky, RegNet: Centre for Regulation and Global Governance, Australian National University

"Harry Glasbeek outlines the bias that is built into our laws and regulatory regimes, which favour capitalism and render it legitimate. The lofty sounding 'rule of law' and the status granted to lawyers and legal reasoning drives a belief system in which the logic of a layperson loses all credibility. *Capitalism: A Crime Story* provides readers with an analysis of the legal justifications used to replace moral and ethical values with the crimes of corporate capitalism."

— Margaret Beare, professor of law and sociology, York University and author of *Criminal Conspiracies: Organized Crime in Canada*

CAPITALISM

A Crime Story

Harry
Glasbeek

BETWEEN THE LINES
Toronto

Capitalism: A Crime Story

© 2018 Harry Glasbeek

First published in 2018 by
Between the Lines
401 Richmond Street West
Studio 281
Toronto, Ontario M5V 3A8
Canada
1-800-718-7201
www.btlbooks.com

Every reasonable effort has been made to identify copyright holders. Between the Lines would be pleased to have any errors or omissions brought to its attention.

LIBRARY AND ARCHIVES CANADA CATALOGUING IN PUBLICATION

Glasbeek, H. J., author
Capitalism : a crime story / Harry Glasbeek.

Includes index.
Issued in print and electronic formats.
ISBN 978-1-77113-346-3 (softcover).—ISBN 978-1-77113-347-0 (EPUB).—
ISBN 978-1-77113-348-7 (PDF)

1. Corporations—Corrupt practices. 2. Corporate power.
3. Social responsibility of business. 4. Capitalism. 5. Corporation law. I. Title.

HV6768.G537 2018   364.16'8   C2017-907080-0
                                             C2017-907081-9

Text and cover design by David Vereschagin, Quadrat Communications
Printed in Canada

We acknowledge for their financial support of our publishing activities: the Government of Canada; the Canada Council for the Arts, which last year invested $153 million to bring the arts to Canadians throughout the country; and the Government of Ontario through the Ontario Arts Council, the Ontario Book Publishers Tax Credit program, and the Ontario Media Development Corporation.

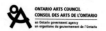

It was the blind and insensate Greed. It was a monster devouring with a thousand mouths, trampling with a thousand hoofs; it was the Great Beast—it was the spirit of Capitalism made flesh.

—Upton Sinclair[1]

Stupidity comes in many forms. I'd like to say a few words on one particular form that I think may be the most troubling of all. We might call it "institutional stupidity." It's a kind of stupidity that's entirely rational within the framework within which it operates but the framework itself ranges from grotesque to virtual insanity.

—Noam Chomsky[2]

A way to
fight back

What is remarkable and a little hurtful to me, a lawyer focused on corporate wrongdoing rather than the intricacies of corporate law and ordinary corporate practices, is that what I (and a relatively small number of like-minded academics) do is thought to be a non-serious thing to do. Real corporate law scholars and practitioners concentrate their efforts elsewhere. To them, the questions of legal personhood, of limited liability, of the relationships between the corporation and outsiders, of the relationships between the corporation and its board of directors, executives, shareholders, and creditors, are front and centre. They subject these issues to deep analysis to determine whether the existing legal regulation of the corporate world attains its objectives, namely, to create optimal conditions for capitalism, for the private accumulation of socially produced wealth. The private accumulation process is seen as unproblematic; indeed, it is portrayed as furthering the public good.

From this vantage point, students of corporate wrongdoing are perceived to be scholars looking for a niche, odd bods seeking to gain notoriety by setting themselves apart from mainstream scholars and policy-makers. The latter are preoccupied with the operations and machinations of an institution, the corporate firm, which plays a pivotal and positive role in our political economy. We, the others, are perceived by them as voyeurs looking for aberrant behaviours. At best, our preoccupation with the wayward is seen as dilettantish; at worst, as unwarranted and harmful. After all, as corporations interact with every aspect of our lives, it is inevitable that they will collide with the interests of others and that, on occasion, these collisions may involve wrongdoing. These predictable, if unwelcome, outcomes should not be given much weight when assessing the utility of the corporation. The conventional view is that corporate capitalists' wrongdoing, undesirable as it might be, is abnormal. In this essay I want to confront that debate-stilling logic.

That logic gains much of its strength from the way in which law allows capitalists and their corporations to position themselves within it. The law goes out of its way to fortify the view that the creation and operation of the corporation is a mere piece of legal technology by means of which lawful and useful ends may be pursued by virtuous actors, namely, capitalists. If any of them offend the law, they will be held to legal account as would any other actor. Capitalists and their corporations are under control. Law's prestige (derived from being seen as a class-transcending institution, as being above politics), renders this starting point uncontroversial, seemingly unassailable. The point of departure of this piece is that this position is assailable and that it should be assailed. It is only if law's rather well-hidden assumptions and pretenses are not confronted that it makes sense to propagate the authorized wisdom.

Law is able to serve capitalists and their corporations so well by contorting the very principles that give law its standing as a legitimator of the status quo. Occasionally, the twisting and turning of law threatens to become plain to the public. Recently, there has been a good deal of public fuss about (what lawyers and accountants like to call) tax minimization. It is aggravatingly obvious that rich people and large profitable corporations are not paying enough tax.[3] Most of us who pay taxes tend to be more than somewhat offended by the fact that some very well-to-do corporations and people engage some very high-priced help to help them park their profits in a low-tax-rate jurisdiction (via cyberspace, of course). There these profits can be deployed to make more money while not paying much tax. If, and when, some of this money is repatriated, it will be taxed at a much lower rate than if it had been taxed in that home jurisdiction before it left.

What happened? We (the people and our governments) were not paid what we democratically decided we should get from enterprises whose existence we nurtured, facilitated, and subsidized. We now have to get those monies from others (ourselves) or forego some programs we democratically had determined we would deliver. We feel that we have been robbed by people in expensive suits and suites. It feels like theft. Theft is committed by a person who intends to deprive another permanently of her property. Those capitalists and corporations and their high-paid help fully intended to deprive us of those monies, permanently. Yet, the legal powers-that-be say that, *technically*, this is not theft. Indeed, the term used to describe these practices, "tax minimization," is used to emphasize their legality. In a revelatory moment, then-president Obama said that tax minimization may not be illegal, but it must be wrong. Apparently he felt badly about this and was saddened that he could not do anything about this unfortunate legal state of affairs. His is the kind of frustration that motivates those of us who think that there is too much wrongdoing in corporate capitalism to look for ways to have it punished a great deal more than it is.

Why, then, is tax minimization not a crime? Because the law says it is not. What the tax minimizers' well-dressed and sleek advisers are able to do is to push the letter of the law to absurd extremes, absurd because the pushing will, as it is intended to do, negate the well-known goals of the law-makers. It is, then, the use of law that frustrates us. It is the law's moulding and bending until it is out of shape that offends us. This kind of legal distortion, this kind of legal manipulation occurs in many other spheres of economic activity.

What is most aggravating is that, despite the frequent denials of people's expectations, law, as an institution, remains unsullied. It retains its prestige as the one institution that, as Ngaire Naffine observes, can present itself as "an impartial neutral and objective system for resolving social conflict."[4] What should be a gaping chasm between law in practice and law's self-portrayal as a neutral arbiter is papered over successfully. The way this works is by building into the very fabric of law assumptions that favour capitalists and their corporations. These assumptions form the unarticulated starting point for lawyers, judges, legislators, and their policy advisers who have to make and apply laws. The resulting applications and formulations of law can be presented as to-be-admired neutral acts, even as the overall impact is to benefit capitalists and their corporations disproportionately.

Sometimes the manipulators go too far and threaten to bring the sophisticated pro–corporate capitalism conjuring into view. Thus it is that, as the tax-minimization practices have hit the news during difficult economic times, they have created a palpable malaise in the public. Less spectacular distortions of the supposedly intrinsic neutral nature of law do not ruffle enough feathers often enough to be as politically significant. For the most part, sleight of hand keeps law, and thereby, corporate capitalism, safe. I am setting out to show how this trick is done. The goal is to give bite to the never-quite-snuffed-out potential for these largely unseen machinations to undermine law's claim about its devotion to the norms and values that give it its prestige and standing. This, it is posited here, could help anti-capitalists' struggles.

The idea, then, is to find a way to fight back. The conventional wisdom is willing to live, and demand that we live, with capitalists and their corporations who push the letter of the law to its extreme. Lawyers characterize such stratagems as good lawyering. It makes sense to ask those defenders of the status quo to accept the analogous efforts by anti-capitalists to push the values and norms that give law (and thereby the corporate capitalism it facilitates) its legitimacy, to their extreme. *They* push the declared letter of law; *we* should push the purported spirit of law. Essentially, the argument being made is that, if the norms and values supposedly held dear by law's functionaries, by lawyers, judges, legislators and their policy advisers, are taken seriously,[5] much of currently accepted corporate capitalist practices will be seen to be wrongdoings, even when there has been no violation of a specific law. The nature of the conduct will be as offensive to our shared norms and values as would be the commission of recognized crimes.

From this vantage point, wrongdoing by capitalists and their corporations will come to be seen to be so prevalent that it will be more accurate to describe it as normal rather than aberrational. This will lay the basis for an argument that corporate capitalism, in legal terms, is criminal *in nature*. On such a revised platform for public debate, conduct engaged in to advance corporate capitalism's profit-maximizing project should have the burden to prove to us that it does not constitute a legally prosecutable crime. If this argument can be put on the political agenda, it should bring two benefits. One is incidental: it proffers an opportunity to think about the nature and role of law in a capitalist political economy. The other is more direct: it should provide those who think that capitalists and their corporations are toxins in the body politic with new weapons as they engage in battles to remove the poison from that body politic.

Law's self-portrayal

The argument is not that the law instrumentally sets out to favour capitalists and their corporations over everyone else. Law could not fulfill its primary functions if it was so blatant. It is more subtle. In Anglo-American jurisdictions, law portrays itself as the institution that protects liberalism. Its stance is that it is dedicated to the maintenance of liberal values, values that posit the equal sovereignty of all individuals and eschew the notion of coercion of any kind. This is reflected in the repeated claims of devotion and adherence to the rule of law. In line with these thrusts, law is wedded to fair processes and neutral applications of the law by neutral (and neutered) adjudicators who treat all individuals as equals before, according to, and under the law. As law is both created by the state and provides the mode of exercising state power, it plays a role in ensuring that that state's inherent coercive power does not undermine the goals of law and its liberal project. That coercive state power is kept in check by judges and constitutional bills of rights. More directly relevant here, as the state is the only legitimate repository of coercive powers in a liberal polity, its use of those powers to punish errant citizens, its powers to treat them as criminals, is sought to be contained by law and its attendant processes. Implicit is this crucial liberal legal proposition:

No one person or institution may exercise coercive power to advantage themselves at the expense of others.

It is an attractive, seductive message that helps maintain an ideology that gives law and, thereby, the institutions it spawns and the activities it controls a difficult-to-challenge authority.[6] Adherence to the ideal of liberalism permits law to legitimate actors, such as capitalists, their corporations and their activities, that it promotes and then regulates. Social historian Douglas Hay observes that law is the rhetorical and instrumental mode by which the powerful both justify and enact their predations.[7]

Yet, potentially, the principle that no individual or institution should coerce any other creates an ideological bind for capitalism and capitalists. In a capitalist political economy, individuals strive to accumulate socially produced wealth and to retain it as their private wealth. Notionally, the actual producers of wealth (workers) could agree to the private appropriation of that wealth by non-producers (capitalists), but if we posit that non–wealth owners have the same need to preserve their interests as do the owners of wealth, it is more likely than not that they would rather keep what they have produced for themselves. They have to be "persuaded" to give up the wealth they produce, no easy thing to do. This "persuasion" may be—indeed, is likely to be—directly or indirectly coercive. Coercive, anti-liberal practices by the powerful are probable. In principle, law should inhibit coercion. Corporate capitalists need to counter the potential of a resultant legal blocking of their drive to grab wealth produced by others. They have a need to have their daily practices seen as compatible, rather than as conflicting, with law's liberal prescriptions. They need to bend law to their ends. They have had a large number of successes on this front.

I already have noted law's characterization of capitalism's principal vehicle for the private accumulation of socially produced wealth, the for-profit corporation, as a mere technical aid to facilitate the much-desired economic growth by which economists justify existing economic policies. Even if, for the sake of argument, it is momentarily stipulated that the corporate firm makes a positive contribution to economic growth (a dubious claim[8]), its legal structure should be anathema to liberal philosophers and market purists because it is likely to lead to coercion. In functional terms, a corporation is a collectivity of people and capitals, marshalled and co-ordinated in a manner that enhances the private accumulation of socially produced wealth. Yet, law has it that it is just an individual like any other individual, merely a convenient tool used to facilitate economic activities between individuals. Only if this legal pretense is accepted can the corporation be said to be compatible with the ideological liberal consensus. And shockingly, this pretense is widely accepted.[9] The largely unchallenged presentation of the corporation as an individual normalizes its participation in market activities. Its pursuit of profits is no more troublesome than that of human individuals engaged in market-eering. Its actions in its own interests are to be seen to be just as virtuous as those of Adam Smith's butcher, brewer, and baker.

Portrayed in this way, corporations are not a clear and present danger to the essential notions of a liberal polity or a free market economy, even though *collectives* are usually seen as a menace to the ideals of both liberalism and the market. After all, it is angst about the threat that collective power presents to the autonomy of all individuals that motivates courts and legislators to limit the right of workers to form unions. It is well known that workers have had to engage in fierce struggles to be allowed to form collectives to advance their causes. The spirit and letter of liberal law stood in their way. Their victories on this front have been hard-won after many bloody extra-legal battles and remain legally contingent. As individuals, workers were poorly placed to safeguard their interests. As collectives formed to oppose individual workers from competing with each other, they have gained some countervailing power. The legal scope given today to unionize is best described as a privilege, rather than a right. By contrast, the right to form a corporation is virtually unrestricted.[10] The legal eagerness to call the capitalists' collective, the corporation, a person, and the equal antagonism toward collectives made up of workers, of non-capitalists, has immense impacts.

To take but one illustration: when workers, trying to get a better deal, claim that they will withdraw their labour in concert, that is, when they want to use their legalized right to strike, they must give notices (leading to delays) and engage in voting processes to get members' approval (leading to more delays and allowing opponents, including employers, to raise objections and to create difficulties). The justification for these constraints is that workers' collectivism, because it is collectivism, is anathema to liberal philosophy and law. The law sees it to be its obligation to control the exercise of such increased unnatural powers. Of course, liberal law cannot prevent individuals, as individuals, from withholding their labour. As individuals they are sovereign beings and entitled to dispose of their assets as they wish. But when workers do this it rarely presents a serious economic threat to an employer. Workers' power rests on collectivization. On the other side of the fence, the law, understanding that it would obviously be unfair to put fetters on strikes but not on the equivalent employer bargaining tool, the lock-out, puts notice and timing requirements on employers (but not the voting requirements imposed on unions ere they call a strike, as employers are always seen as sovereigns responsible for their own business). In this way, law is positioning itself as neutral, which, of course, dovetails with its posture as a class-transcending institution. But this proclaimed neutrality is a mirage.

As law equates an individual worker with an individual employer, the right of any single employee to withhold her capital investment, namely her labour power, allows the employer to withhold its capital investment. This means that the most powerful capitalist weapon of all, the right not to invest inorganic property,[11] is left intact.[12] The procedural equality of the strike and the lock-out thereby becomes a fig leaf that hides law's protection of an economic imbalance that permits coercion of workers by employers. This is a simple instance of how the letter of the law is permitted to fly in the face of the spirit of law's liberalism. The treatment of a corporation as an individual, with all the capacities of any sentient human being, works to the advantage of capitalists. It rends the fabric of law, whose spirit is to be animated by liberal tenets that posit human beings as linchpins of the system. It is a gross capitalism-favouring distortion, but it should not be a surprising one. It does not require much theorizing to understand that a dominant class will mould law and ideology. In the words of Cape Breton miner and activist J.B. McLachlan:

> When kings had divine rights, then king-law was the go. When the church ruled, then church-law was the proper thing. When landlords ruled, then laws were made for the benefit of landowners. When capitalists rule, the right thing is to make laws for their especial good.[13]

In a capitalist political economy, law strives to satisfy capitalism's need to allow individuals to accumulate socially produced wealth, even if this runs counter to vehemently proclaimed ideals. Law has a need to mask its servility to the dominant regime ere it jeopardizes the legitimacy it gains from positioning itself as the primary safeguard of liberal values. As long as it is able to do this successfully, it is able to aid the hegemony enjoyed by capitalism. Law has to be nimble.

The flexibility of legal reasoning

Legal methodology assumes that law is based on fundamental principles that reflect our shared liberal values. Over time, a set of legal rules has emerged that gives life to those liberalism-supporting principles. The rules need to be open-ended enough to be adapted to resolve conflicts and disputes that, while they seem to belong to a genre of previously resolved conflicts and disputes, present new wrinkles. The necessary adaptations are left to law's functionaries, who see themselves as being committed to the fundamental principles undergirding the rules being applied and reformulated.

The contests between lawyers as to how flexible a rule is, the length to which it may be stretched or must be confined, demand special skills and expertise. The exercise is deliberately kept beyond the general public's understanding. The public is asked to believe. It is vitally important to the legitimacy of law as an institution that the public be convinced that the resolution of disputes depends on a trusted professional class's application of rational criteria, not on the status or political power of the disputants and certainly not on the predilections of any of the professional litigators, administrators, and adjudicators. Once this belief is instilled—aided by the mystique and cultural presentations of the trial processes found in film, television, plays, and books[14]—the outcomes, even if unsatisfying to one or more of the parties in conflict, are to be accepted by them because society, as a whole, perceives the dispute to have been resolved in a time-honoured rational and objective way.

Judicially declared and administered law, then, is to be respected because it constitutes a rational decision-making scheme, one not interested in the needs or desires of any one person or pressure group. Law does not acknowledge the existence of classes with irreconcilable differences; it assumes a broad consensus and, within this framework, it rejects the notion that might makes right. Law assures everyone that it is single-mindedly devoted to ensuring that everyone will be subjected to principles and rules that reflect society's consensus about the values and norms that make us a cohesive society, a society whose members are not divided in any profound way. Capitalists and their corporations, therefore, will be subjected to the same principles and rules as everyone else. The approach is that, as members of the consensus, there is nothing inherently wrong with their actions. The nature of their actions is to be determined on a case-by-case basis by neutral and neutrally applied law and by professional functionaries. There is no need to pay any attention to the nature of capitalism or to the question of whether any of its workings or outcomes are intrinsically illiberal, incapable of being justified in a liberal polity. The conduct of capitalists and their corporations, as that of any other actors, may be adjudged acceptable or anti-social. This is how law positions itself—but it is not how it works.

As they argue about how a particular piece of conduct ought to be treated, lawyers and judges draw lines and categorize. They make arguments about what principles and rules of law are most apposite to resolve a specific conflict and then, using established rational criteria, choose among those relevant principles and rules that, legally, might be applied. The elasticity of the system entrusted to lawyers and the courts allows for different outcomes in similar cases. To outsiders, it all looks somewhat arcane and, on occasion, haphazard, but the fact that, sometimes (if not all that often), capitalists and their corporations will be held to account as if they were ordinary folk endorses the idea that liberal law does not privilege capitalists.[15] A few examples will do to

make the point about the apparently open-ended nature of law
and its actual bias.

Sweetening pots and/or bribery

Frequently, corporations or their functionaries feel they have to
persuade some others, who are in a position to do so, to help
them win a contract. Liberal and market principles, positing a
level playing field, do not permit entrepreneurs to use bribery
to gain opportunities that thus will be lost to non-bribing competitors. But, to lubricate the workings of commerce, law does
permit the payment of commissions to those who help locate
people with contacts, access, and influence. Despite law's holding
out that decision-making is based on looking back to established
traditions and on the use of rational criteria, drawing the line
between a permissible commission and an impermissible bribe
does not depend on any obvious legal principle. Thus, while one
is legal, the other criminal, it is unsurprising that law-makers and
courts find it hard to get angry even if they think a payment falls
on the wrong side of the line. To them, a bribe is not an instance
of anti-social behaviour as much as it is an error in judgment
in the way a particular capitalist has chased profits. Indeed, the
Supreme Court of Canada noted that, until it got too embarrassing and the legislature was shamed into changing the law, courts
would routinely allow bribing corporations to characterize fines
as costs incurred when chasing profits, enabling them to lower
the amount of their earnings for income tax purposes,[16] in the
same way as the cost of purchasing income-yielding equipment
could be offset against the calculation of taxable income. It was
seen as just another cost of doing business rather than the kind

of deviance that spoke to any tendency in capitalism to engage in anti-social, anti-market conduct. This kind of line drawing is revelatory about the degradation of ethical values and behaviour in a capitalist political economy.[17] It produces curious results.

The governor of the State of Virginia and his wife were given a Rolex watch, twenty thousand dollars' worth of designer clothing, a ten-thousand-dollar wedding gift, fifteen thousand dollars to offset wedding expenses, and a fifty-thousand-dollar loan by a man whose business it was to market a nutritional supplement. The governor introduced him to Virginia's secretary of health and human resources and hosted a lunch featuring the donor's company; at the lunch, its products were given out for free. The governor asked university researchers to consider doing research into the product and suggested that the government's health advisers should meet with the supplement maker's representatives. To the public, the gift-receiving governor's behaviour must have seemed a straightforward case of betraying all the values it has been taught to believe are sacrosanct. It smelled of corruption. A prosecutor agreed and brought charges to that effect. The Supreme Court of the United States ruled, 8:0, that it was normal for a politician to act on behalf of constituents to solve a problem or to facilitate an undertaking and that such worthy conduct would be inhibited if the circumstances before it were considered to constitute corruption just because the constituent showed largesse to the politician (which the politician had so gleefully accepted). Findings of corruption, said the justices, should be reserved for those cases in which politicians accepted gifts when acting in their official capacity, something the governor had not done.[18] It is plain that this kind of extremely fine, quite exquisite, line drawing shows a willingness to tolerate behaviours that the public undoubtedly would see as tawdry and unethical.

This value-and-norm-threatening approach is pervasive and pernicious. It troubled the dissenters in the famous *Citizens United* decision[19] where they also had to deal with the threat to democratic institutions by people with money to spare:

> Corruption can take many forms. Bribery may be a paradigm case. But the difference between selling a vote and selling access is a matter of degree, not kind. And selling access is not qualitatively different from giving special preference to those who spent money on one's behalf. Corruption operates along a spectrum, and the majority's apparent belief that *quid pro quo* arrangements can be neatly demarcated from other influences does not accord with the theory or reality of politics.

Yet, this understanding that the line drawing is, to say the least, other-worldly, did not trouble any of the justices of the Supreme Court in the Virginia governor's case, nor the majority of the justices in *Citizens United*. In the upshot, there are endless complaints in the U.S. that the electoral system is now corrupted as the wealthy, via their corporations, exert undue influence over the system.

Corrosion of truth as a valued value

At best, then, our judicial leaders, and thereby the legal system, have very muddled visions of ethics and morality. They are willing, in the name of some perceived need to be practical, to draw lines, to categorize. All too often that line drawing favours corporate capitalists and dilutes ethical norms supposedly dear to law and the larger public. Thus it is not surprising that, when faced by an argument that fraud had been committed by a person who, acting on behalf of his employer to sell some of its property, had lied both to his employer and to the buyer, a court ruled that, as it was not unusual for parties to a commercial transaction to lie, misleading and deceiving were not to be classified as criminal actions, unless the lie went to what the court called, but did not (and presumably could not) define, a material issue.[20] This dovetails with a decision of a British Columbia court that determined that, while a vendor had misled the buyer by omitting to tell him that some of the landfill he was purchasing was radioactive, this deceit was not the kind of deceit that deserved an award of punitive damages. The judge said that it was merely the "ordinary kind of commercial deceit" one should expect.[21] He was, sadly, reflecting a verity: law has educated us not to expect the truth.

Advertising

This same principle is manifested by the way law treats the half-truths, omissions, and exaggerations that make advertising effective. While our law-makers emphatically declare that a market economy depends on honesty and fair play and that misleading advertisers deprive ethical marketeers of their rightful share, the ensuing law criminalizing misleading advertising shows an enormous tolerance toward factually empty or fact-distorting portrayals of a product or service. Most of the intentional misdirection (often sought to be made more appealing by relying on not very hidden sexism and racism) is treated as mere puffery, as harmless boasts, rather than unethical efforts at deception.[22]

Legal standards for capitalist morality are low, much lower than those embraced by citizens as they relate to their families and neighbours and live their daily non-commercial lives.

This is the stuff of law:[23] some unprincipled refinements give legitimacy to behaviours that, in a more thoughtful world, would be deemed unseemly. The logic that underpins this phenomenon is not that of liberalism, not that of the moral/ethical precepts we claim to share, not even the logic of the market, the economic machinery to which we claim to adhere. Rather, the logic is driven by the need to maintain and perpetuate capitalism's project. Two illustrations, one old, one contemporary, should make this clearer.

Capital combinations versus worker combinations

From a liberal political and market economy perspective, a combination of assets and talents may be classified as an unacceptable conspiracy to defeat basic individual competition principles, or seen as a meritorious effort at co-operation designed to improve competitive efficiency. This discretion about how to classify conduct has been used to further capitalists' dominance. From the mid-nineteenth to the early twentieth century, the highest courts in our lands did not permit workers to combine to augment their economic clout and use the resulting combination to better their terms and conditions. During that time period, however, the same courts were adamant that owners of wealth should be allowed to combine their efforts to beat out competitors. In one such case, an association of shippers had told an agent that, if it continued to support a competing non-member of the association, the agent would never receive any further contractual work from the association, likely leading to his ruin.

The threat by the shipping association to the agent was a means to deny its competitor access to the market. Its members were employing the then judicially prohibited union tactics of interfering with an employer's unfettered access to labour pools. In the shippers' association case, in startling contrast to its holdings in analogous trade union cases, the House of Lords held that the non-association member did not have any rights against the combining competitors. The judges were not shy about their reasoning. They said that all that the shipping association's members were doing was to look after themselves and that, as long as they did not hit anyone over the head with a metal bar or act with such violence, they were behaving as they should. If a capitalist could not grind his competitors into the ground by economic force, why, capitalism itself would come to a halt:

> [I]t is impossible to suggest any malicious intention to injure rival traders, except in proportion that as one withdraws trade that other people might get, you, to that extent, injure a person's trade when you appreciate the trade to yourself. If such an injury, and the motive of its infliction is examined, and tested, upon principle, and can truly be asserted to be a malicious motive within the meaning of the law that prohibits malicious injury to other people, all competition must be malicious and consequently unlawful, a sufficient reductio ad absurdum to dispose of that head of suggested unlawfulness.

For unions to hurt others when acting in their own interests was actionable; for capitalists to do so was not. Neither pristine legal reasoning nor honest adherence to shared values and norms could explain this kind of contradiction. Only the privileging of the capitalist regime, regardless of other goals and values, could. In due course, this law-destabilizing situation was, as it had to be, redressed somewhat (although unions have never been given the leeway combining capitalists have). Those reforms do not affect the point being made here: law's manifest willingness to manipulate and to let itself be manipulated to attain capitalist goals that may very well offend the spirit of law itself.[24]

The second illustration is provided by the fact that, however troubling combinations and collectivizations are to law in general terms,[25] they do not worry the legal system at all when capitalists pool their resources to form corporations. This is categorized as a desirable, indeed a benign, use of resources and people.[26] As we shall see shortly, the economic power arising from this kind of pooling of people and resources to create an integrated collective may well be very deleterious to the idealized autonomy of individuals. For the moment, merely note what every member of the public knows: economic power is tied closely to political power and, inasmuch as economic power is increased by combining one's wealth with that of others, corporations present a clear and present danger to the idealized notions of a liberal polity. The bribery/political funding issues discussed briefly above furnish evidence of this well-understood potential for the erosion of democratic institutions. More, corporate capitalists may well be able to force legal institutions and politicians to treat them differently to the way in which other members of the public are treated. The recent subprime mortgage scandal and the failure by governments to put the wrongdoers out of business because they are "too big to fail"—indeed doing the opposite by using public funds to help them live—are a testament to the power wielded by wealth concentrated in corporations. Law was not an impediment to this privileging of one set of actors over others. Its ability to twist and turn is not to be underestimated.

Let us turn to one more set of tools available to law to advance the cause of capitalism, even if this means distorting the principles of liberalism it espouses and from which it derives its legitimacy. It is a variant of the categorization technique.

Choosing between spheres of law

Over time law has created pigeonholes in which to slot behaviours in order to pronounce on the right and wrong of them. Contract law, tort law, regulatory/administrative law, and criminal law have overarching principles that coincide. In each of these spheres of law, a standard of behaviour is set (in contract law by the parties themselves within the confines of statutorily regulatory norms); in each, a violation may lead to redress for the injured person(s). In each of them the goals of the law are the same: specific deterrence, general deterrence, restitution, punishment/retribution (in civil law, that is, in contract and tort law damages may be augmented when it is felt that the wrong-doer's conduct justifies it), and a reassurance of the public that order and stability will keep potentially harmful, self-seeking behaviour in check. Victims and legal enforcers choose which pigeonhole to use. Civil, administrative, and criminal actions may be available to them contemporaneously. In any one case, different items on the menu might be selected by different actors pursuing their own interests. Private complainants, public prosecutors, and regulators have overlapping and discrete agendas.

In the upshot, harm-causing conduct plausibly might be treated as completely legal; as to be tolerated as basically benign but requiring some monetary adjustments; as conduct that is somewhat wrongful requiring better conduct in the future and, thus, demanding the imposition of some pain on the bad actors or on some of their agents; or as conduct so reprehensible as to demand serious punishment and shaming. Open-ended as this may seem, there is an overall framework within which all the potential decision-makers function. The built-in, seemingly elastic, discretions are exercised on the bases of some (most often unacknowledged, but very firmly held) assumptions that favour the flourishing of capitalists and their corporations. This is a key point in the argument to be developed and we shall come back to it. In the meanwhile, let me illustrate the point by returning to that subject of current public vexation, tax minimization.

Reprise: Tax minimization

Tax minimization is said to be legal by those who have the power to categorize. They do not ask: What motivates the legal/accounting engineers? Is it just their eagerness to practise their craft, or is it the desire to help their masters to do something that is abhorrent to social values? They never get to those questions because they accept three inter-related arguments. The first two of these are the internalization of the notion that some letter-of-the-law arguments are not to be interrogated and, inasmuch as they favour tax minimizers who bring their actions into line with the letter of the law, so be it. This shrugging-of-the-shoulders approach is what offends the public most. These rules, these letters of the law, are the creature of law-makers. It follows that law-makers could change them. But, obvious as that is to the lay person not bewitched by the idea of the inviolability of politically produced formulas, this simple resolution is anathema to corporate capitalism's legal functionaries. This is so because these rules, these tax minimizers' assisting rules, rest on a third argument, a basic structural and ideological one. This argument, being fundamental to the legitimacy and working of our legal system, is treated as a pillar of the legal edifice that cannot be shaken or challenged. As a corollary, any rules that rest on it are, therefore, difficult to challenge. This needs some elaboration.

The first letter-of-the-law argument is dependent on the hallowed (but notionally challengeable) position of the corporation as a separate person. Having established that each corporation is an autonomous individual by dint of simply saying it is, lawyers and judges then refuse to challenge the validity of this breathtaking assertion.[27] It is thought wrongful and dangerous to question this individual corporate autonomy even when, as is the case in the tax-minimization schemes, a corporation is created by capitalists not to be an autonomous self-serving person but to *pretend* that it is an autonomous, self-serving person. The law is saying that, regardless of the obvious motives of the corporate actors, it may not tamper with its own artificial creation. On its face, this is an absurd argument. What those who make it are really saying is that, if law concedes the possibility that separate corporate personhood is contingent, it will open the floodgates and the corporate form will lose its ability to contribute to the general good. No evidence to support that the corporate form adds much to the general good is proffered.[28] In any other field of social science, unverified assumptions of this kind would be deemed, well, unscientific. In the event, the apparent inviolability of legal personhood serves to assist tax minimizers as will be seen from the second, and related, letter-of-the-law argument relied on by them.

The second technical letter-of-the-law argument used to justify not holding tax minimizers to be thieves is that the manipulators did not take any property from us because we never had it. It was always theirs. There could not have been, then, a deprivation of our property by them. Clever, but not convincing. If the tax dodgers had had to pay their tax up front as wage earners do, it would be clear that it was our money that they were now sending to some tax spa. It does not *look* like our money because we believe that, if we took it from them before they had used it, it would lead to inefficiencies. It is ours but we leave it under their control. And we do so because, once again, we are to assume that the public benefits from letting corporate actors do their thing and, once again, this assumption is made without bothering to provide convincing data for making that assumption. To return: the tax minimizers' argument is one that asserts that the fact that is in issue can only be decided in one way. They do not want the question of whose property it is that is being sent to tax havens to be discussed. There is to be no room to dispute the conclusion that the corporations are not taking anything that belongs to us.[29] This circular argument, resting on assertion, should be easy to dismiss. But it is not because it is fortified by thinking that is unchallenged, namely, the ideological and structural foundation on which these letter-of-the-law arguments rest, in particular, the centrality of the institution of private property.

The sacred nature of private property ownership is deeply embedded; it structures the legal system. The need to safeguard private ownership conditions all legal reasoning. No one, not even the state, should deprive anyone of their private property. While the state must be given some coercive powers to govern effectively, these powers must not exceed what is necessary for good governance. The state's coercive powers should be fettered and it should fetter itself. The pivotal nature of the starting premise that no one, not even the state, may tamper with private property ownership led the Law Reform Commission of Canada to conclude that one thing was certain. No matter how it was to be decided what ought to be criminalized, theft, defined as the intentional permanent deprivation of property, was the paradigmatic crime in capitalist political economies.[30] Thus, a central duty of the state is to prevent theft, and not to engage in it. This is why Justice Wilson, widely considered one of the more progressive judges during her term as a Supreme Court of Canada justice, found that a law imposing taxes was not just an administrative rule but a criminal law, one whose reach should be limited to protect taxpayers from the might of the state. After all, taxes take away property owned by taxpayers. This starting point makes the formalistic, technical arguments used to hold tax-minimization schemes to be legal more plausible than they otherwise would be.[31] The rather logically flawed technical claims that legal persons, including corporations, should be allowed to exercise total dominium over their property gain credibility because they rest on the single most important value of liberal and capitalist law, the right to exclude others from one's property.

Unaware of the hold this hidden premise has on lawyers, judges, and law-makers, ordinary folk out there are not impressed. They are asked to accept the uses made of the letter of the law about which they know so little; they are to acquiesce when they are told that the rules of law are properly monitored and kept in line by trusted legal professionals. The public and the media only see incomprehensible contortions and machinations that spirit away expected revenues. Like president Obama, everyone knows this behaviour is shameful, that it is wrong.[32] But formally, it is not deviant. It is ugly, anti-social, avaricious, unpatriotic. But legally, it is not criminal. How did we get to a position where ugly, anti-social, avaricious, unpatriotic conduct (considered "clever" by the rich, by their lawyers and accountants, by regulators) is not deviant, certainly not criminal? These questions are not just raised by the fuss around contemporary tax-minimization schemes.

Much unsanctioned conduct may be just as ugly as that which the law thinks worthy of criminal punishment. Such tolerated behaviour may be ugly because of the outcomes, because of the harms and injuries it inflicts; it may be ugly because, while the conduct is legal, it abuses the apparent spirit of a solemnly enacted law as, say, in tax-minimization cases, or insults the premises of liberal values by, say, apparently legally providing cheap cotton clothes made from cotton picked by enslaved children in Uzbekistan or by having coerced children digging in the Democratic Republic of Congo's soil to find the base materials that make our legally sold laptops and smartphones work, or by mining and processing asbestos for years after it was known to the manufacturers and mine owners that it killed, or by pouring mercury into a river basin inflicting horrible diseases on Indigenous people whose lives and cultural existence depend on that basin, or by digging for precious minerals in needy countries and relying on local police/paramilitary/army personnel to ward off protestors, by force if need be. And so on. Rarely are these kinds of behaviours treated as offending civil legal rules, let alone as being crimes.

This is what frustrates critical scholars and anti-capitalist activists who try to understand and improve corporate behaviour. We are morally outraged by the seeming institutional indifference when it comes to the misdeeds of the rich and powerful. Some of us want such laws as exist monitored and enforced better and we look for more stringent legal controls. Scholarship on corporate deviance looks for, or discusses, ways in which corporate actors violate standards imposed by law. The usual questions are: Why do they do this? How could they be educated not to do it? What kind of punishment, if any, should be imposed? How should permitted actions be defined? Perplexed and bemused by the rather obvious inefficacy of the legal regulatory schemes, some try extra-legal persuasion. They attempt to get corporate actors to be more like the rest of us, unincorporated as we are. They want corporate actors to be more ethical, more aware of responsibilities to other members of the society in which they operate. Often these suggestions are accompanied by arguments that efforts to satisfy stakeholders other than shareholders will help, not hinder, the chase for profits. But as the illustrations above and a cursory look at the world around us show, not much seems to be working. We struggle because we fight from "within"; we start off with a demand that law apply its ballyhooed liberal principles evenhandedly, treating similar conduct similarly. We keep on hitting our heads on the same brick wall because we accept law's and its functionaries' assertions that there are no unarticulated capitalism-favouring assumptions that affect the interpretations of law's view on how to attain the objectives of the liberal values and norms embedded in the system. While angrily, and often persuasively, pointing to letter-of-the-law technical contortions, we tend to ignore the assumptions that give them bite, rendering regulatory laws and the pleas for social responsibility toothless.

Consider the following scenarios:

A mugger holds a person up and threatens her: *Give me your wallet or I will beat you to pulp.* It is a crime.

An employer says to a worker: *You have asked for lung-saving ventilation but, if I put it in, I cannot make a reasonable profit. I will let you keep your lungs if I can take some of your wages back.* This is not a crime.

This difference in legal characterization is only understandable if we see that, without declaring that they do so, law's professional functionaries feel that they can approach these seemingly analogous situations differently because their thinking is conditioned by not-to-be questioned assumptions about how the world works and should work. Here it is argued that, if these assumptions distort the law's self-proclaimed liberal values and norms, the assumptions should be identified and rejected by those responsible for the maintenance of law as the primary site dedicated to the preservation of a liberal polity and market economy. They should be rejected because they contradict the core of law as a liberal institution. This is what I meant when I began this piece by saying that we, the critics of corporate capitalism, should insist on taking the spirit of law, rather than its letter, seriously. The claim I make is that, if this is done, it will be possible to describe many of the daily practices of capitalists and their corporations as criminal *in nature*, even if not always criminal by the letter and formality of law. This will only be possible if we can make conventional wisdomeers apply liberal law as it should be, and would be, applied if its rules and doctrines were not perverted by unarticulated and distorting assumptions. If this case can be persuasively made, corporate capitalism will be much harder to defend. I now go on to make a preliminary argument to show that it is possible to make such a case, relying on law's own pronouncements and methodology.

Bases for criminalization in a liberal legal system

We know what to do when a crime has been committed. The police look for a perpetrator who committed the offending act with an appropriate intention. Charges are laid and a trial follows. If there is a conviction, a sentencing process is set in motion and punishment is inflicted. Policy-makers and academics use the data generated to ask questions about why such crimes are committed, what social or economic contexts or personal characteristics play a part and how this might help design policing practices, sentencing regimes, social and economic planning, medical interventions, the provision of different educational schemes, and the like. It is all very complex, but we do have a plan of action. We are less sanguine, however, when it comes to the manner in which we ascertain what kind of behaviour ought to constitute a crime.

In *R. v. Vasil*,[33] the Supreme Court of Canada was asked to determine whether a charge being prosecuted required the application of the criminal law burden of proof. The question before the Supreme Court, therefore, was whether the law under which the charge had been brought was merely regulatory in nature, even though, like any garden variety criminal provision, it provided for punishment if a violation occurred. If it created a regulatory offence, as opposed to a criminal one, the burden of proof required to convict the violator was to be less demanding. In legal parlance, the issue was whether the offence described a *malum in se*, that is, an intrinsically bad act and therefore a crime, or a *malum prohibitum*, a wrongful, but not so bad, act and therefore the proper subject of administrative control. The use of that kind of language suggests that courts will know a true crime when they see one. This is untrue. The Supreme Court in *Vasil*, having been asked to say how it defined a crime, put in a valiant effort before it threw up its hands. It fretfully held that, when a law creates an offence and it attracts a penalty when a violation occurs, the offence will be a criminal one if it is written into the *Criminal Code*. This attempt at definition is bereft of persuasive logic. How was it decided that the conduct should or should not be in the *Criminal Code*? Yet, unsatisfying as it is, many observers think the Supreme Court of Canada's approach

pretty well describes the state of play when it comes to determining whether behaviour should be treated as a crime. Nils
Christie avers:

> Crime does not exist until the act has passed through some
> highly specialized meaning creating process and, in the core
> case, ended up as occurrences certified by a penal law judge as
> the particular type of unwanted acts called crime. Crime is one,
> but only one, among the numerous ways of classifying deplor-
> able conduct.[34]

Viewed in this way, classifying conduct as criminal is a
descriptive exercise, rather than a normative one. From time
to time, highly placed judges acknowledge the lack of principle
governing the task. In a decision called *Proprietary Articles Trade
Association* v. *Attorney-General (Canada)*, one of the common
law's luminaries, Lord Atkin, wrote:

> the criminal quality of an act cannot be discerned by intuition;
> nor can it be discovered by reference to any standard but one: Is
> the act prohibited with penal consequences?[35]

This says that it is the kinds of processes selected to deal
with conduct that speak to what view we have taken of conduct.
Perhaps this is why, in public discourse, it is the nature of the
processes used to deal with the infliction of harms that attracts
attention. It underscores the importance that is to be attached
to harm-causing conduct. Popular culture and the media con-
vey the significance and fascination of the procedural rules—the

presumption of a charged person's innocence, her right to remain silent, the lack of any requirement of the charged person to prove anything, the need for police and prosecutors to establish reasonable grounds for searches and seizures, the onus on the state/prosecution to be fair to suspects and to give all necessary information and cautions, the state's duty to bear and meet a hefty burden of proof—all these requirements are known to give criminal law its distinctiveness.[36] If those processes and rules are invoked, it signifies that the harm-causing conduct by the charged person is assumed to be criminal. This tends to ward off questions about how it was determined that these processes and rules should be applied, that is, about how it was determined that particular conduct should be criminalized in the first place.

Thus far the argument is that the initial decision as to whether to deem particular conduct to be a crime appears to be a variant of what I have chosen to call the technique of categorization used by law, that is, of the practice of politics hiding under a legal veil. It does not jibe with law's claim that it is based on liberal principles and the application of rational criteria. Unsurprisingly, vigorous rejections of the above analysis are proffered.

Central to these counter-arguments is that, while there may be grey areas, there is a principled approach to the definition of crime. One major claim is that law and morality are closely linked in a liberal polity. One of the consequences of this linkage is that, given the gravity of being labelled a criminal, conduct should not be classified as criminal if it is not immoral. Of course, it is not every immoral act that is to be criminal. It must be, in the well-known formulation of Lord Devlin, conduct that fills us, as reasonable members of a society with shared values and norms, with "intolerance, indignation and disgust." If this could be said to be a firm guideline, it could be maintained that there is a normative approach to defining criminality, one that is principled and allows rules with rational criteria to be developed. But there is little that is firm about the Devlin approach.[37]

Moral attitudes are continuously pushed and pulled by changing social, political, economic, and cultural factors; they are being moulded and shaped even as they seem embedded. It is not easy to be sure what, at any one moment, the shared morality of society is. To base law-making on a view of what a reasonable person views as morally right and wrong is, at the very least, problematic. It may be safe enough to aver that killing (when not defending oneself or provoked in some extreme manner or not ordered to kill by the state), physically assaulting others, and unauthorized taking will be held to be reprehensible by reasonable persons at all times. Beyond that, things get tricky. After all, the legal moralist position is that only conduct that deeply offends the mythical reasonable person should be criminalized. Some immoral acts should be treated as vices rather than crimes because, while they trouble us, they do not profoundly disturb us.[38] Very quickly a contested terrain comes into view and nuances evolve to deal with the definitional difficulties.

There are those who, wanting to confine the reach of criminal law, argue that only immoral acts that lead to harm of individuals and their property should be considered candidates for criminalization. Others plausibly contend that criminal law should be used to stop people from harming themselves; others go further and suggest that it might be deployed to help people develop a better moral character. Each one of these ways of linking morality to criminality will mean different things to their advocates. To put it politely, when it comes to determining what a crime is, liberal moralism provides a rather elastic framework. Compare, for example, the tolerance shown to the manufacture, sale, and consumption of tobacco, alcohol, sugar, and coffee with the vigorous campaigns to persecute and prosecute the manufacture, sale, and consumption of heroin, cocaine, crack, and ecstasy. Very little is written in stone; very little appears to be principled. The push and pull of populism is manifested by the current debates in many jurisdictions about whether, and if so, how, to legalize the sale, possession, and use of marijuana. There is controversy as to whether the possession of any prohibited drug intended for personal use should be seen as a permissible lifestyle choice or as conduct that reveals character flaws that society must outlaw. Similarly, the sexual preferences and practices of individuals will be tolerated by some as personal biological traits and choices or as mere inoffensive vices, while other segments of the public and law-makers will insist on their criminalization. The emotional debates as to whether assisted suicide should be decriminalized or as to whether a woman's decision to have an abortion should be stigmatized as a crime are addressed and determined differently in Anglo-American jurisdictions, even as they share an understanding of the fundamental principles of common law. This reflects the debates within the debates about the meanings of shared morality, about the nature of the needed connection between moral norms, harms, and criminal law in a liberal polity.

By now it should be hard not to have some sympathy for those charged with defining criminality. Vapid as judges may be when they say a crime is an act that is prohibited by the *Criminal Code* and/or attracts certain processes inapposite to non-criminal behaviours, it is easy to see why they cannot be confident that any one breach of an alleged moral standard that causes harm should rightfully be determined to be a crime. It is a morass. Unsurprisingly, some theorists, as Hart did during his debate with Devlin, argue that criminal law should not be seen primarily as a means to enforce morality. The contention is that harm and the prevention of harm is central to the issue of when to proscribe conduct; its inherent nature as seriously immoral, mildly immoral, or moral is a secondary matter. Laws criminalizing behaviour, then, are to be promulgated in the public's interest in security, safety, and the general well-being of citizens. These advocates, therefore, would label a declared offence to be a criminal one, even if it was not found in a code or set of laws labelled "criminal law." One of the doyens of English criminal law, Glanville Williams, writing about the sphere of the supposedly non-criminal regulatory laws, noted that "one might have thought it impossible for any judge to hold an offence carrying a possible prison sentence is not criminal in any sense."[39] But it is well known that judges, policy-makers, and law-makers do draw distinctions between such laws and true criminal laws. Characterized as being tools to regulate to-be-welcomed behaviours, violations of regulatory laws that attract penalties are not to be seen as so offensive to our shared value system that they merit the stigmatization that criminalization of violators brings; nor does the state need to be so seriously fettered when enacting regulations as its use of its coercive powers in those cases will not impose its moral imperatives on free individuals.

Seemingly, there are no a priori principles that help determine into which category of law any such conduct-controlling provisions imposing penalties should be slotted. The elasticity, the lack of any overriding principle, allows conduct to be subjected either to regulatory/administrative law or to true criminal law control. Complicating the task of classification is the fact that, once a rule is passed to prevent harm, it may become immoral to violate the standard set by that rule. It will be seen as immoral, in part because obedience to a properly enacted law is seen as a moral imperative, and in part because, once conduct is forbidden, the public may come to see a violation as a breach of agreed-upon values; for example, the use of a newly proscribed drug quickly comes to be seen as immoral. It is very difficult, then, to say how we decide that conduct should be classified as criminal. Morality and harm prevention are linked in unspecified ways; resort to Latin tags such as *malum in se* or *malum prohibitum* may make the task seem scientific, but they are in fact substitutes for reasoning.

This all-too-crude sketch of some of the parameters of the debates that have preoccupied some of our most sagacious philosophers, lawyers, criminologists, and other social scientists should suffice to make one point.[40] Neither legal moralism nor the prevention of harm, nor any unspecifiable combination of morality and harm, is all that satisfactory as a determinant of what conduct should be categorized as criminal. In our context here, this indeterminacy, this understanding that we do not have much of a handle as to what constitutes criminal conduct, makes it hard to maintain the bald assertion that corporate capitalism, as a regime, is criminal *in nature*. But some of that difficulty disappears if we shift the emphasis away from the hard-to-pin-down shared moral values of society or the protection of public welfare as the bases for criminalization to another element central to law's political project: the maintenance of the liberty of the individual.

Law is to safeguard the autonomy we all are presumed to have as de jure equal sovereign actors. Law wants each of us to be allowed to do our own thing. It encourages initiative, especially if it is aimed at maintaining or enriching ourselves. This freedom (note the word: it speaks of liberty, a sphere of non-coercion) to act and think as we choose is constrained by the fact that such action may impair the scope of others from engaging in similar, but competing, ways. Law must balance our interest in advancing our own absolute autonomy against that of equal others doing likewise. Some coercions by one sovereign actor of another are always treated as crimes because they violate the sacrosanct autonomy of individuals. Thus homicide, robbery, rape, burglary, and embezzlement all involve the use of force against the person, the taking by direct force or by stealthy fraudulent means. While it is persuasive enough to think of these acts as criminal ones because they offend the mythical reasonable person's view of our moral values or cause unacceptable harm, they are also behaviours that interfere with the liberty of the victims. Each of these acts takes away the victim's autonomy. It does so by coercion and coercive takings. There are many other circumstances in which this occurs.

Much of the remainder of this discussion shows how many of corporate capitalism's "normal" practices flout the anti-coercion spirit of liberal law. They are, it is argued, putatively criminal *in nature*, even if the current technical requirements of criminal law might make prosecution difficult. Worse, law positively assists this undermining of individual autonomy without it being established that the public interest justifies it in doing so. The burden of the argument here, then, is that liberal law normalizes illiberal practices by relying on a series of arguments and assumptions that it hides from view. The hiding is necessary because law's self-proclaimed values are being negated by its tolerance of daily coercions.

Let me return here to the comparison made between the mugger who menaced another person and the employer who negotiated with workers who wanted to breathe safely. It is only if we assume that the mugger was behaving coercively and the employer non-coercively that the two intended takings of another's well-being, the attacks on their autonomy, could be categorized differently, one as a crime, the other as normal behaviour. The lack of consent in the first case and a grant of consent in the second is assumed. It is, on its face and as I will establish below, an implausible assumption to make. If assumptions of this kind are stared down, capitalists and their corporations will have to rely on empirical claims to justify the privileged treatment they get under law. They will have to prove that the harms they inflict by their coercion of others, unlike those inflicted by the muggers of the world, are "worth it." In that setting, a different kind of politics, one that has not been legally laundered, becomes possible. I will now move on to point to the kinds of assumptions and twists and turns that are made to allow liberal law to pretend that, in a corporate capitalist society, it is only outliers, a few bad apples, who spoil the barrel filled with apples that respect the sovereignty and autonomy of all individuals. Once these governing assumptions and contortions are identified, anti-capitalists may be better armed than they are. They should be enabled to make it much more difficult for capitalists and their corporate tools to justify themselves.

Coercion by means of formal, directly enforceable labour contracts

The work-for-wages relationship lies at the core of modern capitalism. Variously talented, but resourceless, members of the working class must sell themselves to those with resources, to would-be employers, in order to live.[41] A central feature of a capitalist political economy is the grossly unequal division of the ownership of the means of production. Just now, this is obvious. Occupy Wall Street and Thomas Piketty's timely book *Capital in the Twenty-First Century* have led even the most conventional of commentators to acknowledge that a few, a very few, have most of the world's wealth.[42] This imbalance gives the wealthy, among other powers, the potential to force those who need employment to acquiesce to their demands. This potential is exploited by employers, who are actively assisted by law.

The legal deal of the work-for-wages contract starts off with the assumption that the employer is entitled to retain the value produced by the workers it co-ordinates.[43] This is portrayed as normal, as agreed to by the wage earners. This portrayal rests on a grossly fact-distorting assumption. It is so erroneous that law is forced to soften its impacts. It does so without ever admitting how inappropriate it is to make the assumption in the first place.

It never rejects the assumption, putting workers behind the eight ball as their protections can be attacked. This is supported by another distortion of reality about the nature of the work-for-wages contract, namely, that the employment contract should be seen to be a variant of the ordinary commercial contract that allows a free market economy to flourish.

A commercial contract between a willing buyer and purchaser is treated by law as a voluntary one between sovereign individuals. The terms and conditions of the agreement should not be questioned by any outsider, not be second-guessed by anyone, not even a court. Sovereigns are free to negotiate whatever terms they like and, in the absence of fraud, duress, oppression, unconscionability, or any other "fraudlet" that would negate the consent to the agreement, the contract is to be enforced.[44] It is assumed that workers (as the equivalent of sovereign sellers of a product) must have voluntarily consented to let employers, after they have paid workers an agreed sum, to take what those workers produce. The most cursory evaluation of the bases for this assumption brings its frailty into view.

In the commercial contract setting, the principals, the buyer and the seller, bargain about objects, money for goods and services. In a contract of employment, the buyer and seller, that is, the principals, are the employer and the employee. But the object of these principals' contract is one of them: the employee, as a person, is the subject matter of the contract or, at least, part of her is. The seller of labour power is selling some of her capacities, her physical and intellectual abilities, her imagination, her dexterity, and so on, the many things that make her an individual, a sentient human being. Pretending that the employer has bargained to buy an object distinct from the person with whom the bargaining took place, and applying ordinary commercial contract thinking to such a bargain, has a perverse effect. Employers are given potential power to *force* their workers to use their capacities to suit the employers' desires, just as they would be able to subject and bend any object they have bought from a willing seller to satisfy their personal whims. And liberal law, law that self-consciously claims to support the inherent equality of all human beings, deliberately and paradoxically gives employers an astonishing amount of help to reduce human traits to objects, to equipment to be disposed of as it suits them.

Every contract of employment, supposedly voluntarily entered into by workers, imposes a legally enforceable duty on workers to obey, a duty to exercise reasonable skill and care, a duty of good faith and loyalty. The worker is not to talk back, let alone rebel; the worker's only goal is to serve her employer and its goals. This is deeply embedded in our supposedly liberal legal system. As Otto Kahn-Freund put it, the lawyer acknowledges that the hallmark of employment relationships is the element of subordination to which one party, the employee, is said to agree.[45] Canada's Task Force on Labour Relations baldly stated that a superior-inferior nexus is *the* distinguishing characteristic of the employment relationship.[46] Even when workers can protect themselves better by having won the right to engage in collective bargaining (obviously a departure from the individual contract model), workers are required to obey all reasonable orders the employers issue. The notionally sovereign, autonomous workers are repeatedly and expressly told that the workplace is not a debating society.[47] Coercion of individuals and appropriation of

their product remain salient features of legally enforceable contracts of employment, even when laws are passed to alleviate the
burdens imposed by its judicially developed doctrines.[48]

Force and taking—it is the norm. It is not hard to see this if
law's pretenses are unmasked. Take our illustrative mugger who
threatens a person with force: the law is sanguine. He is a criminal.
The employer who threatens a worker with wage loss if she insists
on having clean lungs is treated, by means of a legal pretense, as
merely negotiating terms and conditions of a contract (including those of safety at work) with another equally sovereign party.
This is a momentous and absurd assumption. Yet, all occupational
health and safety regulation begins with this premise, that is, with
the initial thought that, whenever possible, safety at work should
be left to bargaining between private (if unequal) actors. I will
come back to this issue, but the implications are dire for workers.
For the moment, I return to my claim that it is patently false to
assert that workers enter voluntarily into contracts of employment.
Workers have no choice about whether to sell their labour power;
if they are lucky they can choose among some purchasing capitalists. They *must* sell parts of themselves. That is their only freedom,
a freedom that is best described as a freedom they are *forced* to
exercise, an oxymoronic idea if there ever was one. The emptiness
of the pretense is neatly illustrated by C.B. MacPherson's critique
of Milton Friedman's reification of the freedom of contract and of
the consequent need to privilege market capitalism.[49]

The liberals' need to use three-card trickery
Friedman favoured the market mechanism because he firmly
believed that, as an economic system, self-seeking competing

individuals would yield the most efficient use and allocation of a nation state's assets and resources. But, for that goal to be achieved, it was imperative that no one individual should be coerced (especially not by the state) to use her talents and resources in any particular manner and that demands for goods and services reflected the choices of sovereign, unpressured individuals, certainly not those a state might prescribe for them. Freedom to choose is crucial to this model. Coercion from any source is the enemy. He offered a simple example: should a government deny a passport to a person, this would be a political restraint on that person's freedom to move, a serious intervention with liberty; if the government, as part of its economic policy, prevents its citizens from taking currency overseas, it also interferes with people's freedom to move. This time, it would be economic coercion that denied liberty. Friedman finds both political and economic coercion repellent. His preference for the market model does not just stem from its capacity to deliver economic efficiency but also, if its requirements are met, from its capacity to enhance the freedom of all individuals. This condemnation of coercion by a truly committed liberal supports the argument I am making that any kind of coercive behaviour is illiberal and criminal in nature. Thus, when it came to the work-for-wages sphere, pure liberals such as Friedman had a problem: they had to find that such arrangements were not in any way coercive. For them, it had to be the case that the market for labour power allows for individual choices of the kind that the idealized market model dictates. Friedman, therefore, had to see the owners of wealth and the wealthless would-be employees as equally sovereign actors. MacPherson shows that to do this, Friedman uses a sleight of thought, one intended to blind observers to the pro-market argument's inherent flaws.

Friedman assumes that a would-be worker might belong to a family that could satisfy that family's needs. If then one of them made a decision to enter into a contract of employment, she would do so because she thought it was a better way to use resources, not because she was forced to enter one. It would therefore lead to a voluntary agreement of the kind that an efficient market model requires. Rather drily, MacPherson remarks that Friedman's postulates, (a) belonging to a group that (b) could provide for itself, rig the game. What if individuals do not belong to a group that is self-sufficient, that is, what if would-be workers did not belong to any fallback group that could and would (if necessary) provide for their needs? Then a choice to work for another would not be a free one as the needy person would have no other choice. Even before Occupy Wall Street or Piketty, inequality was there for all to see. MacPherson, acutely aware of this, of the on-the-ground fact of grossly unequal wealth distribution, concluded that, despite Friedman's finesse, the market model, by its own (and Friedman's) prescriptions, more often than not will lead to coercive employment relationships.

It is curious that so much effort has to be expended to make this point. It speaks to the powerful hold libertarian thinking has on our consciousness, a hold boosted by law's support for this line of thinking. It is, and always has been, counterintuitive to believe that employers and employees meet on a level playing field. For instance, in 1911, Justice Higgins, the architect of Australia's early capital/labour relations adjustment system and a member of the High Court of Australia, that is, a highly influential professional dedicated to the maintenance and perpetuation of capitalism, wrote that intervention with the freedom of contract doctrine was morally mandated:

> The power of the employer to withhold bread is a much more effective weapon than the power of the employee to refuse labour. Freedom of contract under such circumstances is surely misnamed; it should rather be called despotism in contract ... the worker is in the same position as Esau, when he surrendered his birthright for a square meal, or as a traveller, when he had to give up his money to a highway man for the privilege of life.[50]

Workers' initial fights to roll back coercive property/contract rules

Unsurprisingly, workers resisted the legal gift of free contract-making as it was offered from the eighteenth century onwards. A.H. Ruegg has documented how they fought to have their terms and conditions set by the top-down mechanisms established by the sixteenth-century Statute of Apprentices, ungenerous and disrespectful of human dignity as they were.[51] It was well understood by workers and their allies that the supposedly liberty-enhancing right to enter into free contracts was, in the capital-labour setting, not so freedom enhancing. Rather, it provided the employing class with a tool to have oppressive terms and conditions enforced by courts. Thus it was that, while the judiciary was devoted to the project of making voluntary agreement-making a central construct of a liberal capitalist economy, it came under pressure as it developed its contract doctrines. The judges became aware that their pure contract doctrines would involve them in upholding some very unappetizing agreements between employers and workers. The courts, in their own interest as well as that of the potentially oppressed, had to ensure that such agreements did not become too oppressive, too onerous for workers. One court put it as follows:

> The law of England allows a man to contract for his labour, or allows himself to place himself in the service of a master, but it does not allow him to attach to his contract of service any servile incidents—any element of servitude as distinguished from service.[52]

Similarly, the Thirteenth Amendment to the U.S. Constitution not only bans slavery, which manifestly is not a relationship based on voluntariness, but also prohibits an apparent agreement between free individuals that leads to "involuntary servitude."[53] A choice between service and servility, between servitude and acceptable subjugation, is to be made. Some finessing is necessitated. This kind of nuancing is, as modern tax-minimization practices demonstrate, something lawyers pride themselves on doing very well. But clever though it often is, the finessing is not always convincing. Certainly not in the capital-labour sphere.

Judiciary's stubborn reinforcement of coercive tendencies

Those who have to decide whether a particular employment relationship involves terms that are unacceptably coercive, that is, that constitute servile incidents or denote the creation of involuntary servitude, have been given no criteria that objectively, scientifically, will help them answer this question. This forced courts to make choices, to make political decisions. Over time, as is the wont of legal methodology, these political decisions have come to be treated as unchallengeable precedents that are now followed by judges as if they are not political in nature. They look like principles that can now be applied without risking accusa-tions of bias. But the so-called principles now governing labour relations rest on concepts and an ideology tied to an anti-liberal political philosophy.

To be specific: the duties, the duty to obey, to exercise all reasonable skill, to be loyal and of good faith, that is, to put the worker's interest below that of the employer's, are designed to give employers the capacity to transliterate the intangibles they have bought, the intellectual, emotional, and physical abilities of the workers, into value for the employer. The judicial cant is that, unless there is something explicitly to the contrary, it has been legally established that workers always agree to these terms of employment. But the legal decisions courts are relying on should have no place in a liberal polity or a market economy. Those earlier decisions laying down terms of employment ruled a feudal society, a society where, by definition, the parties to work arrange-ments were masters and serfs. The latter's employment conditions were characterized by servility. They constituted involuntary ser-vitude. They were not, and were not seen as, conditions agreed to between equally sovereign individuals.[54] Today, arrestingly, the courts no longer see these oppressive conditions—the duty to obey, and so on, that date their ancestry back to feudal days—as incidents that make a contract obnoxious because it is servile. This is, to say the least, handy for wealth owners.

The helping hand came from a judiciary committed to the promotion of contract-making as a public good.[55] The law the courts eventually crafted in the employment sphere holds itself out as favouring liberal ideas and ideals at the same time as it maintains anti-liberal, pre-contractual precepts. It proclaims voluntariness *and* allows coercion. To a liberal theorist, in contrast to a feudal landlord or a capitalist cheerleader, this use of legal force to empower employers should be troubling.

Another example of the simultaneous adoration of the liberty involved in voluntary contract-making and permitted degradation of sovereign individuals is furnished by the judiciary's translation of an old criminal action resting on feudal principles into an actionable tort in post-feudal times. For centuries, it was legally prohibited for a master to entice a servant (note the label!) to come to work for him while he was still bound to serve another master. It was seen as taking away valuable property. This made less sense, of course, when workers began to enter into free contracts with employers. Yet, the courts decided to adapt the feudal safeguard to help employers out. They gave an employer the right to bring a civil action, not a criminal prosecution, that is, a tort action, against anyone who induced its employee to break her contract of employment with it. It was not as if the employer would have been without a remedy if this tort had not been grafted into the fabric of contract law. After all, the employer could have brought an action for breach of contract against its defecting employee. But the remodelling of the old crime was designed to be an additional protection for employers. The fact that the feudal idea has been transliterated into an actionable tort (a legal wrong known as inducement of a breach of contract) strongly suggests that the courts still perceive the supposedly emancipated free contracting worker, at last in part, to belong (like a chattel) to the employer. This idea should repel true liberals. It makes sense, however, if we remember the oft-ignored fact that the worker has sold part of herself, alienated it from herself as she might have a piece of clothing she had sold.[56]

This schizophrenia (freedom of contract good, some coercion in contract also good) is highlighted by the development of the tort of intimidation. As workers won some statutory protection against the tort of inducement of breach of contract, courts set out to dilute this democratic attack on the purity of contract. Thus it was that in the infamous decision in *Rookes* v. *Barnard*,[57] it was held that, even if no action could now be brought for inducing a breach of contract, the *threat* to breach a contract (here the threat of a strike should the employer refuse to get rid of a non-union employee) would be actionable. The rationale for this startling view was that a threat to break a contract was akin to an act of violence and, therefore, had to be enjoined. Here we have it: a contract entered into by autonomous sovereign individuals is so sacrosanct that it must be defended by the courts at any cost, in much the same way as courts are determined to protect the physical integrity of an individual from assault. But, when that contract is a contract of employment, it is acceptable for the same advocates of free sovereign choices to impose some conditions, such as that of obedience, to which no self-respecting autonomous individual would agree. It is even implicitly acceptable for the law to characterize a supposed autonomous worker as a piece of property whose unauthorized taking is a legal wrong, a sort of theft.

Workers unionize to offset tenets of
private property / contract

Over time, courts looked more to the form of the agreement (Was it made earnestly between two de jure sovereign individuals?) than to its contents to determine whether to treat it as an enforceable contract of employment. From a liberal philosophical perspective, this made sense. Liberalism does not care about outcomes as much as it does about the processes of attaining outcomes. It ignores the starting points of the parties to an agreement. All that matters is their legal capacity to enter into an agreement.[58] Given the perennial inequality of wealth distribution, this proved inimical to workers.

Political struggles to change the balance of economic power were inevitable. This led to legislative interventions to "even up" the bargaining game. We now allow some unionization; we now provide some legislated standards if workers cannot win socially acceptable terms by their own free and voluntary deal-making. The scope and kind of these protections wax and wane as political and economic fortunes change. When wins are recorded, they are significant worker-friendly add-ons to what unmodified employer-favouring law offers. But because they are add-ons, many of the legislative gains made by the working class are impermanent. The essentially coercive nature of employment remains intact.

Still, the fact that there have been many reforms, that is, many interferences with free contract-making, may suggest to some that the continued significance of the ideological and instrumental impacts of the individual contract of employment is overstated in the argument presented here. To many observers, the contention that workers are making autonomous choices when entering employment contracts holds up because, in the advanced economies where Anglo-American laws rule, many of us (after 180 or so years of fierce struggles) have some protections against the legalized right of employers to use their wealth as a bludgeon. It is fair to say that the modernized employment relationship *looks* more benign than it did, but this may only mean that its coercive nature is more insidious, less easily seen. This may make matters worse, as Oscar Wilde suggested:

> Disobedience, in the eyes of anyone who has read history, is man's original virtue. It is through disobedience that progress has been made, through disobedience and rebellion....
>
> Authority degrades those who exercise it, and degrades those over whom it is exercised. When it is violently, grossly, and cruelly used, it produces a good effect, by creating, or at any rate bringing out the spirit of revolt and individualism that is to kill it. When it is used with a certain amount of kindness, and accompanied by prizes and rewards, it is dreadfully demoralizing. People, in that case, are less conscious of the horrible pressure that is being put on them, and so go through their lives in a sort of coarse comfort, like petted animals, without ever realizing that they are probably thinking other people's thoughts, living by other people's standards, wearing practically what one may call other people's second-hand clothes, and never being themselves for a single moment.... And authority, by bribing people to conform, produces a very gross kind of barbarism amongst us.[59]

The fact is that law maintains the basis for a deeply unequal relationship between employers and workers, even when this is sugar-coated by contingent gains made by the working class. Capitalists and their corporations profit enormously from the retention of the doctrines, ideology, and principles individual contract of employment law provides as a starting point for all capital-labour relationships. It enables them to constrain and, in good times (for them), to dismantle workers' political gains. Here they are aided by the enormous disparities in wealth that law tolerates and maintains.

The more would-be employers can force non–wealth owners to compete for scarce jobs with others as individuals, the more they can exploit their workers, the more of the value the workers produce can be *taken* from them by those employers/capitalists. Capitalists have a stake in preventing workers from defending themselves by forming anti-competitive unions. Capitalists oppose the state when it tries to relieve the plight of workers and would-be workers; they instinctively oppose unemployment benefits, decent minimum wages legislation, costly health and safety measures, social security, and so on. In the last two decades or so, employers in the more mature liberal capitalist economies have been able to turn the clock back and overturn many of these legislative hindrances to their insatiable drive for profits. The bargaining power and social wage of workers has been seriously eroded.[60] Paradoxically, just now, even in mature capitalist economies, the (conceptually flawed) assertion that employment contracts are voluntary agreements between equals is harder to maintain than it has been for a long time.[61]

Employers fight to retain advantages

Employers' drive to isolate and thereby subjugate workers, their drive to coerce workers in order to take from them, is made glaringly obvious by the growth of special labour zones that go by names such as Maquiladoras, Special Economic Zones, and Export Processing Zones. David Whyte has noted that the literature shows that, globally, there may be as many five thousand such special spheres employing some forty-three million workers.[62] They are geographical locales carved out by states seeking capital investment. The scheme is to entice employers to set up their production in a cheaper setting, one not bound by soft-hearted social democratic welfare requirements. The employers are provided with subsidies, anything from relief from taxation and excise imposts; to free, or very cheap, water, electricity, and land; to the suspension of certain labour protections applicable in the employers' home jurisdictions (such as limits on the length of the working day, provision for overtime pay, legislated minimum wages, health and safety protections). The desire to take by economic force could not be more directly, more crassly flaunted. It is all reminiscent of the bad old colonial days when companies had their governments and armies apply different (and harsher) laws to the peoples they were dispossessing, while enjoying the benefits of law and its liberal rule of law for themselves. David Korten, writing about the privateers who, armed with legal immunity granted by a king, subjugated and raided foreign parts of the world, described these outfits as

> the forerunners of contemporary publicly traded limited liability corporations ... legally sanctioned and protected crime syndicates

with private armies and navies backed by a mandate from their home governments to extort tribute, expropriate land and other wealth, monopolize markets, trade slaves, deal drugs, and profit from financial scams.[63]

The parallels are hard to ignore. Perhaps even more directly pertinent to the argument here, note Robert Myles's reproduction of an official memorandum written by Lord Hawick, Under Secretary of State for the Colonies in 1832:

> The great problem to be solved in drawing up any plan for the emancipation of the slaves in our Colonies, is to devise some means of inducing them when relieved from the fear of the Driver and his whip, to undergo the regular and continuous labour which is indispensable to carrying on the production of Sugar.... I think it would be greatly for the real happiness of the Negroes themselves, if the facility of acquiring land could be so far restricted as to prevent them, on the abolition of slavery, from abandoning the habits of regular industry. Accordingly, it is to the imposition of a considerable tax upon land that I chiefly look for the means of enabling the planter to continue his business when emancipation shall have taken place.[64]

This passage underscores the point that not only was it always understood that working for a living involves coercion, it was often overt public policy to enable owners of wealth to coerce and dispossess those without any resources except their bodies and minds. These days, capitalism, claiming that its workings dovetail with liberal philosophical and economic precepts, presents itself as more enlightened. Its cheerleaders would, if asked, agree with most of us that the way things were done (by royally encouraged privateers or colonial offices) in the bad old days was wrong, that it now would be seen as crude criminal behaviour. Yet, as the uses made of special zones demonstrate, venal, forcible taking from vulnerable "others" by some of our most highly reputed entrepreneurs is making something of a comeback, if not quite in the same guise.[65]

The oppressions are the outcomes of contracts concluded in special settings. The workers, the supposedly sovereign individuals who have entered into these contracts, have not done so voluntarily, at least, not in the sense that liberals would like that word to be understood.[66] But law has taught us that we should only challenge the validity of contracts that have been concluded in accordance with law's formal requirements in extreme cases of malfunctions. This starting position allows coercing capitalists in these special economic zones to argue that, upsetting as it might be, like tax minimizers, they are acting within the letter of the law. The practitioners of this brutal form of capitalist production are allowed to pretend that, as they cause unfortunate individuals to suffer illiberal servility, they are not the ones negating the shared values and norms of a liberal polity and its liberal laws.

A counter to the renewed coercions? Human rights

The impacts of this kind of legal formalism trouble those not bedazzled by "legal thinking." B.R. Ambedkar, an Indian political activist and scholar, confronted by stark oppression in India, noted that "slavery does not merely mean a legalized form of subjection. It means a state of society in which some men are forced to accept from others the purposes which control their conduct. The condition obtains even where there is no slavery in the legal sense."[67] But this brute sanity is no match, it seems, for Anglo-American law's power to legitimate the reprehensible. This disconnect between popular sensibilities and law has led to a movement to outflank the logic of domestic property and contract laws that do so much to defend capitalism within a liberal polity. Activists and scholars are reaching out for the institutions and instruments of international human rights.

Their contention is that there are some values and norms that transcend jurisdictional boundaries, histories, and cultures and that serious attacks on them of the kind described above are to be classified as unacceptable wrongs, regardless of their apparent legality. Being forced to work in abysmal conditions or exposed to serious risks to life and limb, the exploitation of defenceless children, the debilitation of environments, the dispossession from land to make way for miners and oil explorers and the oft-associated destruction of natural and cultural environments all are portrayed as frontal assaults on fundamental human entitlements that cannot be waived by formal contractual arrangements or even domestic properly procedurally enacted laws. There is considerable debate about the efficacy and reach of this kind of response to harm-causing conduct,[68] but its invocation suggests that much of the corporate conduct that attracts this kind of response is perceived to be of a kind that could, and often does, impel the indignation, disgust, and intolerance in a reasonable person that, in our domestic settings, lead us to categorize the behaviour as criminal in nature. It is the use of coercion by one party against the other that is being deemed a violation of a human right, and the many manifestations of such abuses of economic power by corporate capitalism strongly suggest that its ravenous appetite to accumulate knows only the bounds we manage to put on it. Its impulses are predatory, criminal in nature. This is more visible than usual when the exploiters cannot claim that they have negotiated the oppressive terms with willing victims.

Cascading coercion— not by contract but by sheer economic power

The hold liberal law has on our imaginations is revealed by the fact that the argument that actionable human rights violations have occurred is easier to make when the alleged oppressor has no contract with the victims. Then contract law cannot play its ideological obstructionist role. In those situations, those who want better behaviour, a more ethical approach, feel more confident and meet with greater success as they challenge exploitation and coercion. There are many such situations, pointing to the cleverness of the employing class and to its unceasing desire to get more for its buck.

Profit-seeking capitalists and their corporations continuously find novel ways to use their power to accumulate, even as they degrade the autonomy of others. While they are more than happy to take advantage of the fact that the terms of voluntary contract-making should not be second-guessed, they are equally content to hide behind the fact that they are not directly using their contract-making powers. It suits them just as well to pretend (here is that word again) that any benefits they get from the oppression of others are not due to any *direct* legal coercion by them. Large corporations, such as Wal-Mart or Disney, can force legions of small suppliers who need their custom to compete fiercely for their right to supply them.[69] The behemoths find suppliers in impoverished countries where workers are desperate and labour and environmental protections are minimal. The outcome is inevitable: those who work for these suppliers are treated miserably. There is coercion locally, on behalf of and impelled by capitalists and their corporations in the geographically faraway advanced economic parts of the world. In the absence of formal legal relations between "our" corporations and the "foreign" victims, law, including criminal law, is not readily available when seeking to put the brakes on these giant exploiters. Imagination and difficult political and legal gyrations are needed to hold these harm-inflicting entrepreneurial practices accountable to our supposedly shared norms and values.

Unsurprisingly (and tellingly, given the claim made about the nature of capitalism), this makes this kind of risk-shifting mode of production attractive to our capitalists and their corporations. Cascading coercion has become a norm of capitalism. The public is becoming increasingly aware of how highly reputed businesses and business leaders, not fly-by-night operators, use their power to oppress people in need, exacting a terrible toll. A few for instances should do. The Rana Plaza building collapse in Bangladesh was worldwide news. The list of retailers who profited from the Rana factory's output by hungry suppliers is a who's who of major merchants. Recently, the International Labor Rights Forum has called on people to boycott the major Swedish clothing chain H & M. It wants the consuming public to pressure the retailing chain to develop safeguards that will stop it from selling clothing that it knows to have been made with cotton sourced from fields on which some two million enslaved children in Uzbekistan work.[70] The Pulitzer Center has reported that the Democratic Republic of Congo uses its powers to force children to dig for columbite and tantalum, the elements needed to produce coltan, a product essential to the working of laptops and smartphones. Carl Gibson, summarizing the Pulitzer Center report, notes that children as young as thirteen, earning less than two dollars a day, work without rudimentary safety protections and that some die from sheer exhaustion because the conditions of work are brutal. He goes on: "Multinational corporations like Apple, Samsung, Dell, and HP all depend on the Congolese mining … as 80% of the world's coltan supply comes from the region … the children have no option … school is beyond the financial means of ordinary Congolese families."[71]

The abuses of power presented here are offered as instances of attacks on freedoms of the individuals, as denials of autonomy and, therefore, as anti-liberal, as human rights violations, as potentially criminal conduct. This characterization becomes all the more plausible because much of the conduct also offends a reasonable person's sense of our shared values and norms, much as is the case when a murder or sexual assault takes away the liberty of an individual. In the cases of special production and supply

chain exploitations discussed above, there is a recognition by
the consuming public that the satisfaction of its (often manufac-
tured) desires have led to unacceptable uses of force, that they
are being made party to coercion and wrongful appropriations.
It turns their stomachs. The proof is in the eating of the pudding.
After the much-publicized Rana Plaza collapse, major retailers in Europe and in North America felt it necessary to develop
protocols,[72] undertaking that they would set up schemes to
ensure that their suppliers and outsourced manufacturing contractors abided by some more acceptable standards. They did so
because they realized there might be a backlash by angered, morally offended consumers and, even worse, by bandwagon-joining
reforming legislative bodies. In short, they acknowledged that
they were perceived as having acted contrary to the shared social
value system, as having offended against our sense of morality.

Why not call such behaviour a crime? Earlier on, it was noted
that a constraint on characterizing behaviour as criminal is the
notion that it ought to be sufficiently immoral. These assaults on
the autonomy of individuals, on the core of liberalism, could easily be cast as conduct that fills the reasonable person with indignation, with disgust, to be intolerable to her. After all, it is this
kind of exploitation that led Pope Francis to label contemporary
capitalism a "subtle dictatorship."[73] Indeed, it is not that subtle:
the examples used in this section are the outcomes of deliberate
legal manipulation and should be eschewed by liberal law. Are
these assaults on autonomy, these blows to our supposedly shared
value system any less criminal because the H & Ms, Apples,
Samsungs, Dells, and HPs can *pretend* that the exploitation of

the vulnerable, from which they happily profit, is not connected to them by formalized legal links? Does anyone—except lawyers and other servile functionaries of capitalism—believe that these large capitalists, respected by governments, opinion moulders, and stock exchanges, do not go out of their way, indeed scour the world, to find the cheapest way to produce goods and services even if this inevitably means the savage repression and injuring of thousands of needy people?[74] Should these giant corporations, whose use of market power amounts to a coercive use of force to enable them to appropriate a larger share of the socially produced wealth, not be held responsible for the inevitable impacts on the physical, emotional, and cultural welfare of countless others? How truly different are these behaviours, in conceptual terms, to a street mugging?

A common reaction to the outcomes of direct and indirect contract-based coercion by large corporations is that the behaviours that lead to them are at variance with the way we are taught to, and desire to, behave. There is a growing danger that a sentiment that much of ordinary profit-mazimization is criminal in nature is likely to be more convincing to more and more people. Corporate capitalism's cheerleaders are ready with a defence. It is that all these coercions and their outcomes, from the more indirect and somewhat less expected harms to the more direct and blatantly likely injuries, are inevitable companions to a system that serves the overall public interest. But where is their evidence? Where is the case made for this, either in theoretical or empirical terms? The next sections examine the credibility of this frequently mouthed defence.

The legal neutering of risk and assaults on autonomy

In a liberal polity, the sovereign individual is king or queen. This meshes nicely with the needs of a market capitalist economy and helps legitimate it. In that kind of economy, the creation of overall welfare is left to the individuals' pursuit of the private accumulation of socially produced wealth. Ignoring the fact that, in a large number of cases, the individuals are corporations, that is, functional collectivities, the picture painted is that individual wealth owners are best left to determine what they want to do with their wealth. They are to decide what to make, when to make it, where to make it, to whom to sell it, what kind of people and skills, equipment, and materials to employ, and so on. Sovereign, autonomous individuals are asked to take charge and to plan how they can enrich themselves. Proudly, this is called a business plan.

A business plan entails a calculation of risks. There are risks of loss for the entrepreneurs and there are also risks created for workers, the wider public, and the environment. If the risks for others can be foreseen and are still taken by the planners, it will be disingenuous for them to say that the materialization of the actually foreseen or reasonably foreseeable risks are fortuitous events, even if the particular way in which, and when, they occur, or the extent of the harm done, might not have been foreseen with precision. Only the specific circumstances of any one instance of the materialization of risk might properly be called a surprise, not the fact that it occurred. When these risks come home to roost, it is commonplace to refer to them as "accidents" or "spills," suggesting that they are totally unexpected and most unfortunate outcomes of the natural and benign pursuit of the private accumulation of socially produced wealth. What is sought to be hidden by such language is that the assaults on individuals and their environments often are calculable and were not calculated. Business planners, that is, capitalists and their corporations, are in a position to affect the rate and level of harms to be inflicted.[75] The better part of valour for them, therefore, would be not to pay overt attention to the risks created for others, establishing a sphere of plausible deniability. But in ethical terms, in moral terms, in terms of liberal ideals, such planned insouciance should not wash away the fact that there was an offence to our values; they had a real chance to take measures against practicably foreseeable risks. This ought to be discomfiting to the believers in the status quo.

The only plausible riposte is to argue that, in most cases, the business planners had not, in fact, turned their minds to the possibility of particular risks being created. But this begs the question: If other contingencies were considered, why not this one? Could it be because there is an implicit understanding that some risks to others can safely be disregarded, especially if no specific legal regulation has been enacted to consider those risks? Here it is to be acknowledged that regulations that constrain corporate profit-chasing activities do exist. But, as was argued when discussing the regulatory platforms that provide for legislatively enforceable collective bargaining and minimum standards machinery, those regulations only modify the fundamental structural relations, even when they are seen to be quite interventionist. They do not question the basic starting point, namely, that capitalists should be allowed, as a matter of principle, to ignore risks they create for others. Law has to interfere specifically to impose constraints on this "freedom." It follows that capitalists remain entitled to dispute and use legal contrivances to avoid such (artificial) state-imposed restrictions on profit-maximization. This brings us back to square one: the assumption is that, unless law forbids the use of some process, equipment, or substance, it should be seen as a permitted activity, equipment, or substance. This creates tensions.

The discussion of the supply chain cases above demonstrated how practices that seem as natural to capitalists as breathing often do not jibe with popular sentiment. The social and political fuss around those cases shows that the wider public does expect serious consideration of the welfare of others, whether formal laws require it or not. They see this as being in line with the spirit of the legal system they have been taught to respect. What is being argued here is that law's principles need to be distorted to treat any resulting harms of risk-ignoring business plans as unhappy outcomes that might need to be redressed but not treated as unacceptable anti-social conduct, not as conduct worthy of criminalization. Law justifies this sidestepping of punishment and stigmatization by relying on an empirically unproved claim.

Pragmatism, says the law, demands a trimming of the sails. But how is it to be determined that some things, some fetters, are impractical, while others are acceptable? By relying on capitalists and capitalist-favouring criteria, that is how. There is no question but that our liberal legal system shares capitalists' self-serving claim that overall material welfare is best provided by leaving the task of generating wealth to the private sector. The built-in, almost theistic, belief is that selfishness leads to efficiency. Individual entrepreneurs are seen as virtuous, both by the entrepreneurs themselves and by law. We, the rest of us, should be grateful for the risks capitalists take with their wealth. These virtuous actors' selfish endeavours should be facilitated rather than hindered. The devotees of market capitalism acknowledge—because it simply cannot be controverted—that law's willingness to promote productive activities by private actors may lead to some regrettable results. After all, risks inhere in all productive activities, no matter who undertakes them. Any mixture of people, nature, equipment, materials, and technology creates dangers. This is a cross that, because of the asserted efficiency of the for-profit motive, we must learn to bear, until it gets way too heavy. Not all of the inevitable risks are to be eliminated, giving business planners a good deal of leeway when they set up and operate their profit-maximizing enterprises. Sadly, this means a price may have to be paid by workers, consumers of goods and services, communities, and our natural environments.

These are some of the steps in the logic that has allowed law to take us to where we are. When risks materialize, our first reaction should be that the harms should be seen as the unplanned outcomes of good behaviour, of innocent behaviour, engaged in by well-meaning (if greedy) actors. They are not to be blamed and almost certainly not to be punished, unless there is damning evidence requiring it. Similarly, the equipment, substances, materials, and technologies used in these benign activities should be considered innocent until proved otherwise. This is how we come to think of the mayhem and catastrophes that

blight the lives of millions of people as "accidents" and "spills."
Take, say, those folk who came into contact with what was considered, by law- and policy-makers (but not by scientists!), to
be innocent asbestos mining and processing; these "innocent"
exposures have led to a toll that currently stands at a hundred
thousand premature deaths worldwide per annum.[76] Quite an
accident. Or take the plight of those living along the shores of
the Gulf of Mexico, where virtuous, welfare-creating drilling was
planned and supported by government and, therefore, treated as
benign; the impacts of just one major explosion and leaks has
been horrendous (including eleven immediate deaths and many
illnesses yet to be firmly linked to the contaminations of water
and soil).[77] Quite a spill.

This matter-of-fact characterization and legal treatment of
horrendous calamities rests on a belief that capitalism is good
for us and capitalists should pursue its agenda to the extent that
law does not prohibit directly. The shared starting point of liberal
law and capitalism to the effect that all productive activity entails
risk is to be taken as a self-evident truth. We must bear the hurts
stoically. But the starting point is only a truth if capitalism's project is unchallenged. It should not be unquestioned: in capitalism, everything is upside-down; a perverse logic is allowed to
govern our lives if it is not interrogated.

Productive undertakings are not risk-neutral. The nature of
the risks depends on why and by whom the productive enterprise is initiated. In capitalism it is by capitalists to maximize
profits. This includes keeping down costs by exploiting people
and environments; it includes creating markets by creating
wants, and refusing to produce to satisfy needs if this is likely to

be unprofitable. Plainly, the capitalist economy creates risks for people and their environments that another political economy would not generate.

An easy example is furnished by Martin Shkreli's abrasive responses to criticism of his firm when it raised the price of a potentially life-saving drug by 5,000 per cent. He argued that the company was not coercing anyone into anything. No one is forced to purchase its drug. This angered everyone within sight and hearing. Public ire is raised because we know that the brazen Shkreli makes capitalist sense, underscoring how, at its core, capitalism is at odds with our values and norms. What he was saying was that the company's economic power to raise prices rested on its unchallengeable right to use its property as it saw fit. The need for its product, like a worker's need for a job, did not render any ensuing contract coercive, certainly not criminal. But this case of oppression, unlike the routine work-for-wages contract, became notorious because the emotion-tugging facts made it clear to the public that the raw use of economic power was criminal in nature.[78] Medical products and aids are life-enhancing and, therefore, we would like to think of them as equally available to all. For much of social history, this ideal was pursued. But, sometime during the twentieth century, on the basis of claims that it would be practical to give monopolies over formulas and techniques to profiteers to encourage them to innovate and invent, we have permitted access to medical products to be controlled by private owners.[79] Access is now subject to market power; need is no longer the central criterion. To underscore how radical this is, note that Jonas Salk refused to take out a patent for the polio vaccine he developed, believing that it should belong to all people;

similarly, the developer of the first synthetic malaria vaccine donated his patent, that is, his exclusive right to make himself truly rich, to the World Health Organization so that all who need the vaccine might have access to it.

It turns out, then, that the claim that universal pursuit of self-ish goals by private actors will enure to the overall welfare of society and that therefore, on the whole, corporations are virtuous and positively contributing actors is a crude one. It only speaks to overall growth in monetary terms. The minuses are taken out of the equation. Some of the minuses are staggering economic and social harms, even as they are the product of activities that add considerably to growth in monetary terms.

Tobacco corporations meet a want (which they have created by successfully marketing and advertising an addictive product) that, in terms of overall benefit to society, has a deleterious impact (as shown by the fact that several governments had success in winning damage suits for losses incurred by increased medical spending on the industry's victims). Asbestos producers and manufacturers continue to sell their toxic product to whosoever will buy it, knowing that it will cause debilitating diseases, painful early deaths, and great economic losses. Arms manufacturers are more than happy to sell their products to buyers who they know will use them to maim and kill many innocent people. Financial analysts question whether gun manufacturers are in a position to take advantage of the expected increase in demand after a mass killing in the U.S. so that they can better advise their clients as to whether to invest in the gun-makers' equities, as everyone knows that mass shootings mean booming sales for gun manufacturers and retailers.[80] All these capitalists' profit-seeking activities add to their wealth and to overall monetary wealth, pluses as long as the negative impacts on society's welfare are not deducted from the "bottom line."

Law's different definition of risk in non-capitalist spheres

Welfare in terms of what people need to be safe and healthy plays no special role, certainly not a central role, in the normal practices of capitalism. If the central goal of production was not profit but the satisfaction of needs rather than wants, that is, if it was to meet people's essential necessities rather than their desires (inbred or stimulated), the business plan of producers (even if still private) would be quite different. Some of the principal needs to be satisfied by the productive activity would be the health and safety of the workers, of their communities, and of their physical and cultural environments. The balance between risk-creation and outcome would be totally different than it is under capitalism. There would still be injuries and harms, but they would be different both in kind and number: the rate and kinds of "accidents" and "spills" would be totally different.

Why would a legal system based on liberal principles not demand such an approach toward wealth creation? Why should it not reject the gross assumption that makes the life of capitalists and their corporations so easy, so legally blameless, even as they daily undermine the autonomy of individuals? Such a rejection would bring law in line with its claimed devotion to liberal values. If law encouraged producers who set out to provide needs rather than wants, if it did not leave goals to be determined by greedy, private accumulators, it could put the welfare and integrity of the prized individual on the highest pedestal. And it would do so directly, intentionally. Producers who did not take measures that showed they valued life and life-enhancing conditions by eliminating foreseeable harms would be considered to be engaged in unacceptable, anti-social behaviour, worthy of criminalization.[81] Liberal law would not be distorted to serve capitalism's project. To the public fed the maxims of neo-liberalism, this line of reasoning may seem far-fetched, yet it has resonance in some spheres of our legal system.

When the autonomy of an individual is assaulted by an actor who is not engaged in what is conventionally seen as a profit-seeking exercise by the appropriation of value produced by others, that is, is not engaged in a capitalist activity, law has little difficulty in applying the principle that anyone who fails to act with respect for the autonomy of others should be stigmatized and outed as anti-social. An example from daily life and familiar to students of criminal law 101 is offered to make the point.

A man drinks to excess and gets into his car. Singing to himself, thinking he is on a cloud rather than a busy road, he kills a pedestrian. He will be prosecuted for violations of various specific road regulations and, most likely, be prosecuted for a species of a more general law such as homicide, criminal negligence, manslaughter, or recklessly causing grievous bodily harm. Like any business planner, he will not have intended any harm to a particular person or to any person. In this sense, he had no animus, no criminal intent. But he will be adjudged to have acted criminally because he was indifferent to human welfare and life. He failed to do what a reasonable person is expected to do, namely, think about the consequences of drinking before he got into the car. In liberal terms, he failed in his duty to respect the autonomy, the liberty, the sovereignty of others. In a business planner's case, the equivalent indifference would be the failure to plan for the welfare of others and that of their environments as they set up the business. Yet the notion that this failure in the private accumulation sphere to respect the autonomy, the liberty, the sovereignty of others is a potential crime appears not to be on the legal or the political agendas of the authorized knowers. It is not there because it is necessary to keep on thinking of selfish for-profit activities as virtuous, as mostly benign. If this was not the assumption, it would become logically necessary to engage in unwelcome interrogations as to whether capitalist relations of production might be just as offensive to our values and norms as gormless drinking drivers are presumed to be. Comparisons that push toward this kind of interrogation must be stopped in their tracks.

To underscore a theme that runs through this argument, note that labelling the drunk driver but not the business planner as a criminal is an upside-down result if the premise is that there need be evidence of a serious moral delinquency ere a crime can be said to be committed. The driver omitted to take care because he was stupid; the business planner omitted to take care to make it easier to make money. Who was the less ethical? Who was more criminal-like in traditional legal and liberal terms? Do the claimed, *but unproved*, overall benefits provided by business planners justify this apparent contradiction? The drunken driver not only imposed costs, but he also, like any capitalist, contributed to some growth in monetary wealth by using an automobile, buying alcohol, generating medical and legal activities, driving the insurance business, and so on. Is there an argument that, unlike in the drunk driver instance, the risk that is presented by a profit-seeking activity is rarely as obvious to the business planner as we take it to be to the drinking driver? The answer must be: sometimes this will be true, sometimes not, a not very comforting answer for those who make the argument that we should assume the virtuous nature of profit-maximizers as our starting point. Should a reasonably foreseeable risk not be on the planning agenda given the gravity of the harm it entails? Consider the way in which this kind of issue was discussed by Lisa Heinzerling in her work on ethics and environmental law.[82]

Law's marginalization of established values and norms when capitalists create risks

Heinzerling lists a whole series of legal judicial pronouncements, legal decisions, decrees, and statutory enactments that support the proposition that the knowing killing of another is ethically wrong.[83] The laws she uses to illustrate her point hold that an ethical wrong is committed not only by an actor who deliberately assaults another, but also by one who knows that there is a practical certainty of death when initiating her actions. Heinzerling relies on this reasoning to go on to argue that it does not make it any less a wrong if the defendant knew only that there was a statistical chance that someone would die.[84] She would not excuse the business planner for a failure to meet this ethical standard simply because they had no animus toward, or knowledge of, the danger to a particular person. In ethical terms, when an individual aims his anger at another and kills, this is, more often than not, a crime of passion, something that Heinzerling adjudges to be less ethically troubling than a crime of dispassion, a label that is apposite to the capitalist's business plan when it pays little attention, if any, to the practically foreseeable injury or death of some unknown persons or persons.

Some outcomes of law's tolerance
for capitalists' risk-creation

Heinzerling does not conclude that this kind of ethical failure ought to lead to criminal convictions, but she believes that for-profit business planners should act as ethical agents. She bolsters her argument about the need to adopt an ethical approach by pointing to the harms that are likely to result from ethical lapses.[85] She notes the extent of some of the actual harms caused by ethical inattention and records that unchecked, uncalculated, but checkable and calculable, impacts of for-profit activities, such as mining, mean that "fine particulates in the ambient air kill tens of thousands of people every year in the United States alone ... 26% increase in premature deaths are attributed to fine-particulate air pollution ... [and that] widely used chemicals such as vinyl chloride pose risks of lethal cancers and other diseases ... greenhouse gases [also have grave impacts on health and welfare]."[86]

There are many similar data that strongly suggest that not taking precautions when there is a practically foreseeable certainty that harm will ensue inflicts a lot of injuries and environmental and other ills on society. Take, for instance, a summary compiled by David Whyte of the U.K. reports on the incidence of health and safety harms. His overview led him to conclude that

managements are responsible—and are legally liable—for the majority of deaths caused by working ... we can say with little doubt that the minority of deaths caused by working can be regarded purely as "misfortunes" or "accidents" which were not avoidable ... *the majority of deaths* at work do not result from "out of control" or haphazard circumstances, but *are the result of decisions or non-decisions that could ... be traced to the authors of those decisions.* [emphases added]

The infliction of potentially foreseeable deaths and harms short of death by routinely exercised inattention,[87] by failures to act as the ethics and morality espoused by an idealized liberal society dictate, is commonplace in capitalism. This should and does create legitimacy problems. To ward these off, a series of interconnected arguments are proffered by corporate capitalism's defenders.

Justifications for special treatment of capitalists' risk-creation

First, it is argued that if behaviour is not legally criminal, it should not be castigated. Ethical considerations are not a basis for interventions with capitalists' endeavours. It is then averred, rightly, that most planning investors do not bear an animus toward any person or thing. They are focused on making their enterprise work. In this sense they have no intent to inflict harm or injury. A central ingredient of criminal law, it is argued, is absent. But technically, this is not all that convincing an argument, given the way in which we think about criminal law. It is a narrow view of the meaning given to intent in criminal law, as the drinking and driving example illustrates. And of course, it reflects a shallow view of the ethical and moral values that supposedly underpin the liberal legal system. A second argument is needed and provided.

Reliance is placed on the well-founded claim that the creed of individualism that anchors each of (a) capitalist relations of production, (b) the principles of the market, and (c) liberal law decrees that no one has a duty to act positively toward anyone else. Colourfully, Justice Deane, of the High Court of Australia, illustrated the principle as follows:

> [B]oth priest and Levite ensured performance of any common law duty of care to the stricken traveller when, by crossing the road, they avoided any risk of throwing up dust in his wounds.[88]

This bald statement of the anti-human relationship between unconnected individuals sums up an essential aspect of both market capitalism and liberal law. It should, and does, shock our conscience. Criminal law 101 uses the example of a passerby who, not wanting to get his trouser cuffs wet, watches a baby drown in a twelve-centimetre-deep puddle of water. He has no duty to rescue the baby. A parent or guardian of the child or a police officer does have such a duty, and would be committing a crime if the child was left to drown.[89] The non-imposition of a general duty to rescue dovetails with a political economy in which letting others starve if they have no resources and cannot sell their labour power, or letting them be deprived of a life-saving drug because the price is too high, are seen as neutral acts. It supports a starting point that tells business planners that they have no positive legal duty to do good over and above any already established legal duty. These business planners, therefore, have an incentive to ensure that any such specific legal requirements are kept to a minimum and have as little impact on them as it is politically feasible to ensure.

The example of the baby in the puddle never fails to horrify students. The lack of respect for life is as pointed as it can be; the ethical/moral lacuna in liberal law is a gaping cavity. Defenders of non-criminalization of the failure to think about others, therefore, cannot just rely on the lack of a duty to rescue. They reach out for yet another argument. This amounts to an acknowledgement that law should, and does, recognize the duty not to harm others and their environments (as opposed to act positively to advance their well-being), but that the scope and enforcement of any such negative duty should be left to be administered by the non-criminal sphere, by the machinery of a sphere where practical feasibility (in terms of market capitalist efficiency) can be taken into account and balanced against the value of life, human happiness, and our values and norms. It should therefore be left to civil law (tort law) and administrative law (regulatory laws) to define and patrol this malleable sphere of regulation. Criminal law should be eschewed. Liberal legal systems, in fact, do impose some duties on capitalists and their corporations to avoid the causation of harms (as opposed to duties to do good). They are found in a regime of laws called regulatory laws.

This argument used to defend the non-criminalization of heedless business planning is one, then, that does not flatly deny the existence of a possible duty to take the needs of others into account when chasing profits, but it is one which, if it is decided that there should be an obligation toward others, dilutes the consequences for the risk-creators when that duty is breached. It is an argument that postulates the need for, and then legitimates, trade-offs between, on the one hand, the enhancement of life and, on the other, money and the satisfaction of greed, a rather fraught ethical and moral stance.

This conscious attempt to classify a duty to take care as not criminal in nature is, of course, a prime example of the legal methodology that I called categorization above. It was argued there, and shown here, to be used by law-makers and interpreters to give an appearance of scientific evenhandedness, while it and they defend unarticulated assumptions that further the goals of capitalist relations of production, an exercise that requires unequal treatment of like behaviours. A web is spun.

Coercion: Statutory regulations that permit assaults on individual autonomy

Rugged individualism and capitalism's need for sacrifices

In form, regulatory laws resemble criminal laws. The central goals of criminal law (deterrence, retribution, and denunciation) are also the goals of regulatory regimes. Yet the perception sought to be created is that there is a huge gulf between these two categories of law. This is crucial to the legitimacy of capitalist activities.

Criminal laws proper are concerned with behaviours that must be stamped out (for example, murder, theft, sexual assaults) either because they are morally repugnant (murder and assault are attributable to anger, revenge, greed, and lust, unattractive values) or because they destroy the autonomy and liberty of individuals. Regulatory laws are not designed to deal with conduct that is thought of as anti-social. They set out to facilitate competitive profit-maximization. As we have seen, the central idea is that harms of some kind are inevitable and that, to satisfy our desire to have wealth generated for all by encouraging individuals to chase wealth for themselves, we must be and are assumed to be willing to sacrifice some of our bodies, lives, and ecology. The assumptions on which we base our regulatory laws embody the crass social Darwinism of John D. Rockefeller:

> The American Beauty Rose can be produced in the splendor and fragrance which bring cheer to its beholder only by sacrificing the early buds which grow up around it.... This is not an evil tendency in business. It is merely the working-out of a law of Nature and a law of God.[90]

Underpinning the system of regulatory laws, then, is the same kind of thinking that leads to the problems that give rise to the need for regulation in the first place. To be specific, it assumes that it is acceptable for capitalists and their corporations to do some injury, to do some harm, to others and their life-enhancing environments. As a leading pro–free market, pro-capitalist legal academic, and now highly regarded judge, Richard Posner, observed:

> Only the fanatic refuses to trade off lives for property, although the difficulty of valuing lives is a legitimate reason for weighing

them heavily in the balance when only property values are in the other pan.[91]

The caution with which the sentence ends is important. It is hard to see how tolerance toward the infliction of some injury, of some harm, as a planned outcome of regulating laws, squares either with our notions of shared values or with the contention that it is not permitted to attack the sovereignty, the liberty, the physical integrity or the life-enhancing environment of another person. For such harm-causing activity not to be seen as criminal, it is crucial that it can be sanguinely said that it serves some tangible, measurable public purpose. Let us take another standard criminal law 101 example to see how we differentiate between conduct that we see as not serving the public weal and similar conduct that we do want to occur.

If a wealthy man approaches an impecunious person and offers him twenty dollars if he will only stand still while the rich man punches him in the nose, and the poor man agrees and takes the money, he may still call a police officer and stop the wealthy man from punching him. The law will say it is an invalid, unenforceable contract, a contract voided because of its moral turpitude. Liberal law, devoted to the autonomy of individuals, forbids us from voluntarily agreeing to an assault. This is why it is necessary for those who promote and engage in violent sports to get a *legal* permit. This gives an exemption to protagonists if they dole out violence within the parameters of the sport's rules. If those limits are exceeded, criminal charges may be laid against the athletes who were too violent.[92] It is plain that the activities are seen as intrinsically criminal in nature, at least in liberal and legal terms, but that the participants are given a free "get out of jail" card in order to let the game go on.

Legal regulation enacted to govern the normal undertakings of capitalists and their corporations resembles the granting of permits to boxers and hockey players: there, a certain amount of mayhem is to be allowed to make it possible for action to occur that the paying public wants to see. Like sporting events, the occasionally harm-inflicting profit-chasing activities are in the public interest and should be given a permit. Regulators of profit-seeking activities have anticipated, have foreseen, that there is a practical certainty of a certain number of "accidents" and "spills." They are intent on lowering the risks, rarely on eliminating them completely. That is, regulations are enacted even as our legal authorities anticipate, indeed, believe with reasonable certainty, that harms will ensue even if the standards they have set are met.[93] The only distinction between these entrepreneurs and boxers and hockey players is that they were not aiming at a particular person. In legal morality terms, to some this may make their actions less obviously reprehensible than planned violence against a chosen opponent in a sporting contest. But in terms of liberal law's respect for the sacred nature of the autonomy of individuals, they also might be seen as worse violations. While the victim of permitted sporting violence may be said to have consented explicitly to harm inflicted within the rules of the sport,[94] this is not obviously the case when a regulation permits violence to be inflicted on workers, on consumers, on communities, or on the environment.

To illustrate: one of the as-yet-unfulfilled ambitions of occupational health and safety regulators is to reduce the overall risk of injury or death in the workplace to 10 per cent. Imagine that a promoter invites sixty thousand people to watch a spectacle for free. To sweeten the offer, the invitees are told that they will be given a free hot dog. The only catch is that, at half-time, they have to remain in their seats while people with weapons will come out and randomly shoot six thousand of them, killing some, seriously wounding others, and inflicting minor injuries on others, lasting psychic injuries on a few, and mere scratches on the remaining victims. If they agree to that, they can keep the hot dog and watch the second half of the show—for free. How full would the stadium be? How many consenting people would attend? It is a bargain that few people with other options to recreate are likely to choose. But there always will be some, with a gambler's instinct, who might do so. How would the law regard their choice? It is a bargain that liberal law should not, and would not, enforce because it is a morally repugnant one; it would be voided by standard legal principles. Yet that is the bargain offered by a regulatory scheme that attains its objective of an overall injury rate of 10 per cent; it is also the bargain made when a regulatory scheme grants legal permission to emit a certain amount of pollutants to fill the ambient air.[95]

There is no principle based on either moral or liberal tenets that justifies such a result. Both the regulators and the profit-maximizers are equipped with the certain knowledge that harm will be inflicted. They set the level of harm that victims are to accept. This should be anathema to a society wedded to the core principle of the sanctity of the individual. To overcome this problem, a highly adulterated and diluted understanding of what true consent means in a liberal society is to be postulated. In the first part of this argument much was made of the way in which law has diluted the meaning of voluntarism in the capital/labour relations setting. The importance of this argument is now underlined. Once that dilution is seen as unproblematic, once a perversion of consent is normalized, callous calculations become the norm. Critics of the profiteers' and policy-makers' large-scale indifference to particulates in the ambient air are likely to be met by the riposte that the public must have consented (implicitly, one supposes) to these risks. No evidence is proffered for such a bald and prevention-inhibiting proposition. For a rather dramatic but not untypical instance of the calculations spawned by the logic of consent to a trade-off of life for money, note that the Ontario Ministry of Labour once decided that, when regulating the use of the carcinogens vinyl chloride and asbestos, the standard should be set on the basis that fifty extra deaths per year per hundred thousand workers was an acceptable level of risk.[96] Presumably (if they followed Posnerian logic) they weighed lives more heavily than profits in their scale and came to their standard by making a finding about the contribution made to overall public welfare by the businesses that use carcinogenic materials.

We will return to the way in which this kind of weighing is done. At best, it is a pseudo-scientific exercise. For now, note the assumption about the underlying belief that workers would be willing to accept this level of risk. Even if workers had participated directly in setting this standard, where is the evidence that they did agree to a risk when it is understood that they entered into the agreement where they had so little choice? After all, they needed a job and a risk-filled one often is the only one on offer.

It is a problem for those who want to justify the status quo. To obscure the difficulty of legitimacy posed by the calculus involved in setting standards that impose hard-to-justify risks, the process is given a sobriquet that makes it appear to be normal, not malevolent. It is referred to as cost/benefit or risk-management analysis. There are refinements and variants of these kinds of analyses but, in the end, they share a single purpose: they are designed to make capitalism viable.

The logic of those proponents of risk analysis is plain enough: just as we want to enjoy sporting spectacles that involve some violence and, therefore, have to give a legal pass to the participants, we must give a pass to capitalists and their corporations if we want capitalism. Law's liberal principles have to be adapted (read: abandoned?). Proponents of both violent sport and capitalism say they are being practical. But in the sport situations, both protagonists are more or less equal, both have a real chance of winning. In boxing, the fighters are to be of similar weights and have exactly the same equipment. In hockey or football, the adversaries are one-on-one, well-trained athletes, and so on. This is why there is so much fuss about performance-enhancing drugs: they undermine the fairness of the contest and, incidentally, the assumed consensual nature to harms inflicted by the contest. None of this is true when it comes to the practice of capitalism. Unlike fighters or hockey or football players, who all run a very similar risk of being the injured party as a result of the violence of their interaction, this is markedly not the case when the risks to workers, consumers, communities, and the environment are created by capitalists and their corporations. Among the two million deaths, 270 million injuries, and 160 million occupational related

diseases inflicted per annum worldwide, a miniscule number
are suffered by employers. Of the millions of people adversely
affected by pollution arising from profit-maximizing activities,
the overwhelming majority are not profit-maximizers. Rather,
they are people who cannot live on top of the hills, away from
the prevailing winds, in wooded lands, or more pointedly, they
are people who live in the economically impoverished parts of
the globe; they are non-capitalists and, among them, the poorest
are likely to suffer the most.[97] In capitalism, the risk of harm does
not constitute an equal opportunity terrain. The risk-creators are
not the risk-takers. In capitalism everything is upside-down. The
point being belaboured is that, even when regulated capitalists
search for profits within the boundaries set by regulations, their
conduct is criminal in nature as they are allowed to continue to
inflict harms on non-consenting individuals. Capitalism's legitimacy should always be in issue.

Legal "justifictions" not to criminalize the sacrifices demanded of non-capitalists

The liberal principles of law get strained to breaking point and its
intellectual defenders have to weave and spin. Thus it is that, as
we have seen, well-informed intellectual defenders of the status
quo take refuge in arguments that our authorized knowers can
tell a *malum in se* from a *malum prohibitum* when they see it. It
explains their resort to the hapless argument that, if a provision
to which a penalty is attached is found in the *Criminal Code*, it
is a crime, and if a provision to which a penalty is attached and
which looks very much identical is *not* in the *Criminal Code*, it
is not a crime. The ambivalence and confusion is also revealed

by some of the language in common use. It is not unusual to see regulatory laws described as quasi-criminal, an obviously imprecise term. In Australia, the law-makers have created a category of civil offences (a nifty, but unpersuasive, way to avoid having to make a decision on the definition of crime) to which they attach civil penalties (a sneaky linguistic trick, if ever there was one). It is truly hard to formulate any principled liberal legal arguments to hold that so-called regulatory laws that look like criminal laws in the formal sense and that share the purposes of such criminal laws should not be treated as having created crimes. For this reason, the defenders of this difficult-to-defend proposition try to forestall any arguments that regulatory laws allow them to continue to engage in conduct that is criminal in nature.

It will be recalled that one of the ways to explain that a law is criminal is by reference to the processes by which it is to be applied and enforced. When it comes to regulatory laws, the processes furnished by the legislators are determinedly non-criminal. All that the prosecution has to establish is that a violation took place, that is, that the physical act or omission occurred. The burden then shifts to the defendant to prove that they exercised a reasonable amount of due diligence to try to avoid the commission of the breach. This clearly signifies that the drafters did not want there to be a criminal stigma attached to business planners who harm the physical integrity of others and of their environments or who unethically rob them of some of their property by, say, some financial finagling, or of their autonomy by forcing them to accept disagreeable terms and conditions. But not too deep in their hearts, the drafters of these "non-criminal" regulations are aware that these business planners are doing something unprincipled, at least, in liberal ethical and liberal legal terms. The due diligence defence they want to afford those engaged in to-be-assumed non-criminal for-profit projects reflects their understanding that the profit-chasers could, and should, eliminate assaults on the welfare of others. It is an implicit acknowledgement that they are in much the same position as the driver who can determine whether to take appropriate care as provided for by the rules regulating highway driving. But to get drunk in breach of those highway standards not only leads to sanctions under those rules because no due diligence was exercised, but may also be perceived to be criminal in nature. Although it does happen, we very rarely ask that other question—Was the lack of due diligence evidence of the commission of a real crime?— when confronted by a deviation from a regulatory standard by a corporation for profit. This is so, even though, as observed earlier, it makes sense to think of the drinking driver as less morally repugnant than the for-profit harm-doer. This dissonance can only be explained away by acknowledging that undue weight is being given to an anti-liberal argument that puts profit-seeking above idealized liberal principles and that this makes good, practical, economic sense.

A fraught empirical defence mounted to buttress legitimacy

At the end of the day, then, those who (successfully for the most part) classify regulatory laws as mere facilitating, administrative, non-criminal kinds of laws are forced to make an appeal to pragmatism. They posit that capitalist relations of production are here to stay and that this is good because its practitioners are virtuous and generate wealth for themselves and welfare for all of us. Inasmuch as injuries and harms are inevitable, they ought to be kept to a minimum and a regulatory regime that does this is producing an appropriate balance between wealth creation and the autonomy of all individuals. It is in the public interest to dilute the spirit of liberal law. This line of argument is intended to negate the claims by impractical people who contend that regulatory laws should be treated as if they were enacted to create real criminal offences. It is essential to this argument of practicality that the regulatory authorities will know when the public interest in augmenting overall welfare outweighs the public interest in not having individual autonomy harmed, that they will know when it is acceptable to allow our shared morality and values to be sacrificed. The idea that they might be able to bring this off is quixotic. Consider the following:

- The balancing to be done continues to assume the virtuous nature of capitalist modes of production; it continues to assume that, in liberal legal terms, they are innocent until proved otherwise. Technologies and substances are innocent until proved otherwise. The weights put in the pans of the scale used to reach an "acceptable" balance are heavier on the profit side of the scales than on the detriment to individuals and their environments side.
- Cost/benefit analyses involve the calibration of incommensurables. On one side, there is the cost of putting in a preventive system, which theoretically can be calculated in dollars and cents. On the other side, it is hard to measure the benefit bestowed by any one productive activity

and even harder to measure the cost of the economic losses suffered by the victims of a materialized risk. This difficulty is compounded by our inability to measure the pain, suffering, or emotional and psychic losses of such victims.

- To add insult to injury, it makes perfect sense for regulators to ask the presumed virtuous, non-criminal risk-creators, the capitalists, what the risks of their operations are and what the practicality of eliminating or diminishing the risks are. This is fraught. Historically, capitalists and their corporations have been indifferent to the costs they impose on others. Nothing is being done in our modern regulatory settings to diminish the capitalists' impulse to emphasize the benefits of their business plan and to downplay the costs they are likely to impose. They are likely to lie. No less a person than Adam Smith told us this:

  > The proposal of any new law or regulation of commerce which comes from this order ... comes from an order of men, whose interest is never exactly the same with that of the public, who have generally an interest to deceive and even to oppress the public, and who accordingly have, upon many occasions, both deceived and oppressed it.[98]

  Such fettering of the adventurism of capitalists and their corporations that does emerge is unlikely to be effective fettering.

- Governments are handicapped. The initial decisions of what to make and what to use are left to the choices of presumed innocent profit-chasers who have all the pertinent information. Governments react, rather than act. Hurt and killed workers, consumers, and users, visible environmental degradation, and disastrous financial losses are the main sources of information for regulators charged with balancing the supposed benefits of productive for-profit activities against the harms they inflict. We get new safety standards when the harms inflicted by for-profit activities become too great, too politically embarrassing to accept. The respect for the autonomy of sovereign individuals reflected in ameliorating regulatory schemes is an improvement from the more ethically and morally debased standard in an unregulated setting but, ordinarily, they are very limited improvements, subject to persistent attacks by capitalists and their corporations.

These starting points—permitting self-interested capitalists and their corporations to set the agenda for politically necessitated regulatory fetters, together with the embedded ideology that capitalism is (a) inevitable and (b) to be promoted—tend to yield rather lax regulatory requirements. Of course, the conventional wisdom does not admit that it is these structural factors that lead to regulation "lite," even as they often do have to acknowledge that, given the history of a particular industry (say, rail transport, as in Lac-Mégantic, or coal mining, as in Westray),[99] more stringent regulatory laws might have been warranted. They go back to their mantra: entrepreneurialism is a "good" that must be nurtured in the public interest, not discouraged. Regulation requires compromise and, therefore, occasional unhappiness with results is inevitable.

The end result is that the legitimacy of regulations is easily contestable by the regulatees, namely, capitalists and their corporations. This makes for great standard-setting and enforcement difficulties. Embedded in these regulatory schemes is the Rockefeller notion that to inflict harm for the sake of profits is not to be thought of as reprehensible. Indeed, the opposite is true as, once again, we hit a wall because, in capitalism, everything is upside-down. It is the inhibition of the chase for profits by inherently coercive governments that is reprehensible, not the unfettered conduct of red-blooded capitalists. The logic this imposes gives credibility to the notion that violators of necessary standards should be brought to their sense by education. They should be counselled and cajoled into doing better; the direct imposition of punishment on would-be straying wealth creators should truly be a last resort,[100] reserved for real criminals like those who steal from convenience stores, sell recreational drugs, or assault people during a domestic dispute. This should be a hard position to defend. The need to do so has given rise to a small army of scholars who compete with each other to persuade policy-makers how best to attain the goal of ensuring compliance with regulatory laws without punishing wrongdoers all that much, certainly without stigmatizing them.[101]

Compromised regulation

"Responsive regulation," "really responsive regulation," and "really responsive risk-based regulation" are just some of the refinements on the theme. What these schools of thought share, however, is much more important than the differences their proponents want to emphasize. There is an unspoken agreement to the effect that the unequal power relations of capitalism are not to be subjected to challenge; to the contrary, they are to be preserved by the regulatory schemes even as this built-in inequality leads to coercions and assaults that liberal law should exorcise. As a for instance, Steve Tombs sharply concludes that the scholarly literature on regulation spawned by the scams that led to the great financial crisis of 2007 and beyond constitutes "a torrent of self-referential banality from which considerations of power, capital, class *and even crime* are notable for their absences."[102]

We are now in a position to see why critics of the way in which we deal with corporate wrongdoing start from behind the eight ball. The governing framework continues to assume that we cannot do without profit-maximizers whose selfish drive for more unwittingly serves all of us. It is their lack of regard for anyone or anything else, we are to believe, that makes them so valuable to society. This allows the position to be taken that their right to omit to take care should be the default position of law and public policy. It is acknowledged that, sometimes, it may be necessary to restrain them to avert some of the harsher human, economic, social, and political impacts of their private profit-seeking regime. Criminal law is not to be the weapon of choice. Civil law is one answer, but regulatory law is the major tool in the kit box. Its aim is to keep capitalism safe from anarchic capitalists and their corporations who might wreak too much havoc and raise troubling political questions about the system. But despite these heroic efforts, those troubling questions are posed again and again.

Pushing back: Putting the spirit of liberal responsibility onto the agenda

Critical scholars and activists rebel against the categorization technique used by mainstream defenders of the status quo. They argue, as foreshadowed, that the acknowledgement that there is a civil and regulatory duty to avoid omissions of foreseeable harms to others can be used as a basis for criminalizing behaviour currently treated as non-criminal. These critics argue that what is now legitimated indifference, could, and on occasions should, be treated as criminal conduct. Employing the categorization technique justified by standard jurisprudential methodology, they seek to redefine crime. Typical is the definition proffered by Pearce and Tombs. They suggest that corporate crime is constituted by

> illegal acts or omissions punishable by the state under admin-
> istrative, civil or criminal law which are the result of deliberate
> decision making or culpable negligence within a legitimate organ-
> ization. *These acts or omissions are based in legitimate, formal,*
> *business organizations, made in accordance with normative*
> *goals, standard operating procedures, and/or cultural norms of*
> *the organization, and are intended to benefit the organization*
> *itself.*[103] [emphasis added]

This suggestion should resonate both with theoreticians and with the public. First, it pays respect to the spirit of law's liberal precepts. Second, it allows for the criminalization of shocking events that fill the reasonable person with disgust and clearly undermine the autonomy of the sovereign individual. Think

Ford Pinto and the more recent, eerily similar, cases such as the GM ignition switches and the Takata airbags; think asbestos, vinyl chloride, mercury poisonings; think Bhopal, Exxon Valdez, BP in the Gulf of Mexico; think Enron, the subprime mortgages, the LIBOR scamming, CommInsure, the ANZ in Cambodia, Macquarie Bank's many admissions of dereliction—all cases in which controlling capitalists and their corporations knew or could have known what the impact of their failure to prevent harms by their underlings would do. All of them behaved like the driver who does not think, or thinks and does not give a fig, before he drinks and drives.

Unsurprisingly, therefore, while conventional wisdomeers cannot afford to accept the logic that underlies the proffered reformulations of crime, on occasion they are forced to take actions that acknowledge that the reforming concept they resolutely reject has real merit. These occasions arise when the outcomes of letting capitalists plan their profit-seeking undertaking in the safe knowledge that they will not be held to account for not doing anything about risks they foresaw or could easily have foreseen are just too dramatic, too horrible. The public indignation then leads to calls for criminalization. Legislators may have to overcome stiff opposition from the dominant class's opinion moulders, but will act to still the palpable public unrest. They feel under pressure to reassure the non-capitalist public that politicians, policy-makers, and the law do truly care about life and the social values by which non-capitalists want, and expect, to live.

Canada's Westray mining tragedy provides an easy illustration. Before the mine blew up, there had been fifty-two violations of mining safety regulations detected by the inspectorate, none of them leading to punishment. In the aftermath of the deaths of twenty-six workers (no employers or managers, of course), a public inquiry was established. The findings were that the operators had been incompetent at best and, at worst, heedless of human life. Note here that, while the violations of the regulations provided evidence for such findings, it was not the lack of obedience to the resultant orders for breaches of those standards that got everyone angry. It was the business plan and the daily modus operandi of the mine owners that was seen as repellent, as worthy of criminalization. This was explicitly supported by the authoritative commission of inquiry.[104] Its recommendation was that, if the law did not allow for criminal prosecution of corporations and of their senior operators for this kind of conduct, it should be reformed. After a lengthy battle (capitalists, their corporations, and their ideological defenders did not like this turn of events), legislation was enacted. It makes it possible to criminalize the omission to take action when it is reasonable for some senior officers to believe that it is likely that there will be a failure to take adequate care (calibrated by regulations or general legal principles).[105] This gradual realization that the usual exceptional legal treatment of capitalists and their corporations needs to be reined in from time to time is not jurisdictionally specific. Analogous legal reforms have been initiated in some Australian jurisdictions and a somewhat less sweeping statute was enacted in the U.K.[106]

These recognitions that heedless risk-creation and risk-shifting, so natural, so routine to for-profit corporations, is potentially criminal in nature and might be so treated go against the grain, go against the starting premise that capitalism's normal workings involve virtuous actors, using innocent substances and methods that may occasionally lead to unfortunate "accidents" and "spills." The resistance mounted by capitalists and their corporations' cheerleaders has been forceful and, thus far, has blunted the impact of the new criminal law reforms. In Canada, after ten years of operation, there has only been one prosecution in respect of fatalities at work per year, even though the number of fatalities has remained constant. The calculation is that there is a 0.1 per cent chance that a prosecution will be launched after a workplace death.[107] That this was always going to be true can be gleaned from the fact that all these reforms took ages to put on the statute books (in Canada close to eleven years; the Australian Commonwealth statute took a similar twelve years to be given life), despite officialdom's caterwauling about the tragic nature of the results that had led to them.

The powers-that-be continue to believe in their internalized make-believe view that it is not unethical, not criminal, for practising capitalists to undertake actions that they know, or should know, will lead to a certainty of death or other unacceptable outcomes. Thus, when confronted by policy-makers under pressure to confirm that we still live in a liberal democratic society and should punish capitalists as if they were ordinary folk, they ask everyone not to be romantic. Pragmatism is to rule. Principle is a luxury. The liberal spirit of law must be bent to allow capitalists and their corporations (and thereby all of us) to flourish. It is not a very convincing argument on which to base a legal system. At best, it is amoral; it asks that we should be willing to suspend our ethical goals for the sake of expediency. In any event, this demand, based as it is on the notion that the suspension of our adherence to our shared values and norms is a practical response to real-world circumstances, is not backed by any sound evidence. What is certain, however, is that the tolerance for amorality, or worse, for ethical and moral failures, does nothing for the social cohesion that any society must have to flourish.

Summation and suggestions for action

Antecedents

The argument made here about capitalism's nature should not come as a surprise. Whatever today's conventional wisdom asks us to believe, capitalism's past is not that of a virtuous system. As capitalism emerged, privateers, financially and militarily supported by governments, were charged with extracting wealth from foreign lands and peoples. The prehistory of corporate capitalism is marked by forceful takings and dispossessions. The predators' exploitations knew no limits.[108] The word "loot" is the English rendition of the Hindustani word for plunder, one that was associated by Indian people with the East India Company, the first multinational of any importance.[109] Slavery was a norm. Edward E. Baptist tells us that slaves were not only used to produce cotton but were also used as collateral for credit obtained from bondholders to finance early U.S. capitalism.[110] And, as Douglas Hay and Paul Craven have documented, when slavery was made illegal in England, the colonial government and its corporations found new ways to enslave whole populations.[111] The history of the savagery, of the brutality, of capitalism is not in doubt.

Today, when assessing capitalist relations of production, we are expected to ignore this appalling record. We are not to think that the pursuit of riches by *any* means, fair or foul, is the defining characteristic of capitalism. We are not to believe that capitalists and their corporations will eagerly seek out ways to shift the costs of the risks they create in order to maximize profits to non-wealth-owning humans and their physical and cultural environments. We are asked to believe that the capitalist beasts of yore that roamed the world in pursuit of hapless prey have changed their spots. The way in which we portray our political economic regime is that, after many political struggles, the citizens of modern capitalist states have won governmental power. They control their own destiny. A democratically elected majority can, acting through a set of relatively autonomous institutions, pursue the interests it chooses. But there are problems. In a capitalist economy, the fear is that a small number of wealthy people might exercise undue influence because, to meet their needs and wants, non–wealth owners are dependent on those wealth owners' investment. There is a known danger that the few might lord it over the many. This danger needs to be averted. Central among the institutions designed to provide the needed counterweight in our jurisdictions is law, more specifically, liberal law.

Law is portrayed, and holds itself out, as the above-the-fray protector of the autonomous individual. It is said to be devoted to liberal, as contrasted to capitalist, ideals. It sets out to enable individuals to follow their own stars as much as that is consonant with the needs and desires of others. Law prescribes, monitors, and regulates the political, social, cultural, and moral environments that reflect the values we are assumed to share and, therefore, have to respect. This legal system derives its standing and legitimacy from applying these undergirding principles, and the rules they spawn, evenhandedly. It gives legitimacy to all actors and activities that comply with the law's requirements and prescriptions. Capitalists, invariably portrayed as individuals, are just that: individuals whose efforts at self-advancement within this regime are to be viewed as unexceptional, indeed as meritorious. Of course, individual capitalists, like any other individuals, may fall afoul of the law, but the practice of capitalism, of individual capitalists chasing their dreams, is not legally challengeable.

The fly in the ointment is that there is daily evidence that capitalism and its practitioners have not changed their impulse to take and to dispossess, by force, by stealth, by hook or by crook. Many of them do not want to, and often do not, act with the respect for others and responsibility for their conduct that law demands of all of us. How can this be if we are capable of bending all actors to our will supported by our legal system?

The blunting of democracy

The most common argument on offer is that large corporate actors have overwhelmed the state apparatus as corporate money has displaced the people's power and law-makers' independence. This is often described as the money-in-politics issue, particularly visible in the U.S., but not restricted to that country. The corruption of the electoral processes by politicians who, increasingly, are seen to be seduced and pressured by those who can make and break them and their causes leads to oft-voiced concerns. There are many exposés of the impact of lobbyists and the enormous influence of think tanks and universities that house respected researchers and personnel and are well funded by large corporate interests. Lobbying has become a major industry. Lee Drutman reports that, in the U.S., corporations spend $2.6 billion a year on lobbying, which is more than is spent on the maintenance of the two Houses of the U.S. legislative branch. The biggest corporations have more than a hundred lobbyists at work. Drutman goes on to observe that not only do lobbyists act negatively to stop regulation, but they also act positively to get legislators to enact measures that suit their clients.[112] The revolving door phenomenon by means of which those state functionaries charged with monitoring and policing large corporate actors are easily manipulated by the hope of becoming employed by the very people they are supposedly watching and disciplining, and the correspondingly frequent appointment of corporate actors to governmental positions where they regulate the sectors from whence they came, constitute a downward drag on governmental capacities to regulate private actors. Lee Fang lists a number of influential decision-makers in the U.S. revenue department who have close connections to some of the major corporate actors who benefit from loose taxation rules;[113] Seamus Milne describes the English situation to be more like a swinging door than a revolving one.[114] Add to all these machinations the assaults on the public delivery of services and goods—the so-called deregulation and privatization movements—plus attacks on trade unions to remove worker resistance, include free trade deals that give large wealth owners more leverage vis-à-vis any one government, and the clout of corporate capitalists grows exponentially every day. This transfer of power from the people and the state to corporate capitalists is furthered by an ever-increasing concentration of ownership of the means of production and finance. For instance, Arundhati Roy, writing about concentration in India, records that "less than one hundred of [India's] richest people own assets equivalent to one-fourth of its celebrated GDP.... Giant corporations virtually own and run the country."[115]

It is easy to see how a case can be made that the liberal democratic institutions, such as law and electoral democracy, become less and less able to subjugate corporate capitalists to the public will, to make them abide by the shared values and norms supposedly embedded in, and believed to be protected by, our legal and political institutions. This is why so often those who feel themselves to be vulnerable to corporate capitalism's profit-seeking adopt a mendicant's position. They plead for more ethical investors. Their hope is to gather enough ethical investors to form something like a critical mass, enabling them to sway corporate decision-making in a more ethical direction. Similarly, they appeal to the good nature of corporate functionaries and call for their voluntary consideration of the interests of stakeholders other than shareholders. The corporate social responsibility movement is vibrant and vigorous but not, as the repeated damage to our values and norms documented here demonstrates, all that effective. These pleas and appeals for nicer investors, more considerate corporate functionaries, rarely result in hard, enforceable laws. This contrasts sharply with the many rules designed to establish better-functioning capital markets and more shareholder protections found in the corporate laws and securities provisions of all Anglo-American jurisdictions.[116]

Corporate capital's apparent ability to enfeeble the political and legal institutions in place to safeguard all of us against the coercive powers of the owners of wealth is the result of a conscious, political fight-back by corporate capitalists. Not so long ago they were concerned about curbs on their exploits and exploitations as non–wealth owners were using their electoral muscles to advance their interests. In the immediate post–World War II period, activists, comforted by good employment conditions and spurred by wartime promises, militated for radical changes. The corporate sectors circled the wagons as the social movements appeared to be gaining ground with their agitation for a post-capital society. Eric Hobsbawm observed that, in an ancient utopian sense, the social movements of the time were revolutionary: they were seeking to establish a reversal of values.[117] Some of the more thoughtful capitalists called for acquiescing to a more inclusive capitalism. They felt threatened. The palpable angst in the thinking ranks of corporate capitalism was well founded. One of these worrywarts, John Paluszek, doubted that the corporation would survive into the next century;[118] one executive thought that corporations were so threatened that the environmental movement might want to protect them by putting them on the endangered species list.[119]

The response to the perceived crisis was to ward off the potentially revolutionary tendencies by making capitalism appear gentler and kinder. To this end, institutions and think tanks proliferated.[120] The impetus was to align capitalist relations of production with the values and ethics of what was posited to be a classless political economy, to push the corporations to accept the need for greater sensitivity, to be more socially responsible.[121] But this never led to an acceptance by corporate capitalists that they should curb their drive to accumulate; it did not signify that corporate capitalists were actually intending to accept lesser profits in exchange for peace and quiet. They were more calculating: it might be sufficient to give the *appearance* of being more caring, more responsible. Jane Anne Morris suggests that, to ward off direct intervention by democratically elected governments, thinking corporate actors set out to educate corporate social responsibility's advocates. The idea was to get them to demand what corporations could afford to give. Her claim is that the recurrent intelligent corporate response to social pressures is to placate, to co-opt and to reframe the demands so that they can be accommodated.[122] Her observations, based on the gyrations of the 1960s and 1970s, appear to hold true today. In 2016, John Lorinc argued that hundreds of multinational corporations are wrapping themselves in the mantle of liberal corporate social responsibility in order to dilute its impacts. "No longer content to be mere delivery systems for profits and goods, the vast majority of publicly traded firms now sell themselves to conscience-stricken investors as enlightened bureaucracies.... Global capitalism is now green on the outside, sooty on the inside."[123]

The movements to constrain the anti-corporate capitalist sensibilities in the aftermath of World War II were supported by a series of powerful and well-publicized supporting manifestoes and strategic plans. A proliferation of scholars, think tanks, and institutions set out to provide an intellectual basis to enfeeble the democratic tendencies that menaced corporate capitalism's project. There was the well-known tract by Daniel Bell, *The End of Ideology*. Its title revealed its agenda: it was designed to convince expectant populations that they should not engage in class war against the dominant wealth owners.[124] There was unabashed advice to the rich and powerful, alerting them to the danger of democracy. Probably the best known of this genre of propaganda was penned by Michel J. Crozier, Samuel P. Huntington, and Joji Watanuki; it was tellingly entitled *The Crisis of Democracy*.[125] It was written as a report to an association of corporate capitalists formed to ward off the assault on corporations. Then there was the highly influential *Powell Memo* (also known as the *Powell Manifesto*), first published in 1971. It was written for the U.S. Chamber of Commerce and provided a blueprint for action to blunt the impact of interventionist governments. Powell became Justice Powell of the Supreme Court of the United States, where, in 1978, his decision in *First National Bank of Boston* v. *Bellotti* laid down the basis for *Citizens United*. It was the first time that any judge in the U.S. opined that corporations had a constitutionally protected right to free speech.

Anti-unions, anti-workers

As the end of ideology was being proclaimed by the intellectual gatekeepers, actual capitalists and their political allies fought vigorous campaigns against trade unionism, generating an avalanche of allegations about the corrupt nature of union "bosses." Typically, they were characterized as entrepreneurial self-seekers, rather than as selfless trustees for their members. This mode of attack was so successful that it remains a major weapon in the pro-capitalist camp's armoury today.[126] Simultaneously, unionists were accused of unappetizing, unpatriotic politics. They were painted as communists and fellow travellers determined to wreck democracy and to bring about regime change on behalf of the working class. That they were being described, somewhat contrarily, as being both venal selfish crooks and highly romantic idealists never put a crimp in the campaigns waged against them. The Kefauver and McCarthy hearings in the U.S. successfully led this two-pronged attack in the U.S. Later, there was the Margaret Thatcher revolution as her governments gave Milton Friedman and Friedrich Hayek's anti-government, pro–private capitalist agenda life, a path to be followed by the Reagan administrations. Both Thatcher and Reagan launched vigorous, indeed vicious, attacks on trade unions (coal miners, traffic controllers). They saw unions as major impediments to their grand vision for the hegemony of market capitalism. They had great success. By 1992, anti-capitalists who, not long before, had sensed that they might have enough power to challenge the reign of corporate capitalism, began to realize that they had lost the struggle.[127] Triumphantly, Francis Fukuyama published his *End of History* essay. Its central message was that societies that had embraced corporate capitalism had come to the end of political and economic evolution. From now on, the only adjustments that would need to be made to this final stage in political economy would be remedial ones required to cure odd malfunctions.[128] It was an academic's way of saying that Thatcher had been right, that There Is No Alternative (TINA) to the current regime.

This sketch of the corporate fight-back against democratic impulses makes it clear that, despite our staunch proclamations that we have empowered the people by the grant of the universal franchise, the state's ability and willingness to use law and its political powers to rein in excessive exercises of power by the dominant corporate sectors are becoming ever more marginalized. Liberal law and electoral democracy are not what we hold them out to be. I have attempted to show here that liberal ideals of law have been distorted, often leading to their near annihilation. Potentially, this undermines the belief that law can be trusted to protect individuals and their shared values and, incidentally, erodes the legitimacy that adherence to the legal ideal could give to corporate capitalism.[129]

Reprise: Empirical justifications for lack of democracy and accountability, restated and rejected

Defenders of corporate capitalism mount a riposte: we are told that the legislative and legal systems are being bent a little, not torn to shreds. The bending is necessary so that democratically enacted law and its ideals are adapted to the "real world." Some minor, practically necessitated, adjustments have been made. We must be practical, utilitarian. I have argued that this response is transparently self-serving. Specifically, (a) the "practical need" justification refers to the needs of capitalists, not to those of their victims, and (b) the "necessary" adjustments made to the edifice of law and its liberal principles are more like a major destruction of the building than minor repairs to it. The law and its foundational principles are bent, twisted, bruised, and battered on behalf of capitalists and their corporations because we are all supposed to agree that law should not stand in the way of prosperity.

To this end, it is simply asserted, it is simply pretended, that the advantages of treating capitalists and their corporations as benefactors as they chase profits are greater than those that could be yielded by an alternative social system that would pay more respect to the physical, political, and cultural integrity of non-capitalists and their environments. Asserting a fact does not make it true, especially not this asserted fact. David Korten observes that growth in GDP "is not eliminating poverty and creating a better life for all ... instead creating increasingly grotesque and unsustainable imbalances in our relationship to Earth and to each other ... humans now consume at a rate of 1.6 times what Earth can provide. Weather becomes more severe and erratic, and critical environmental systems are in decline."[130] Truly, it is hard to believe that anyone (pace Adam Smith) could seriously think that self-serving behaviour would bring well-being to others. As John Maynard Keynes said: "Capitalism is the astounding belief that the most wickedest of men will do the most wickedest of things for the greatest good of everyone."[131]

This is why, despite corporate capitalism's vigorous intellectual and emotional massaging and messages, there is at any one time only a lukewarm acceptance of the claims made on behalf of corporate capitalism that it is not only the most efficient means to bring us bounty but also the most benign. What leads many people not to contest the regime's claim to efficiency is their dependence for their daily sustenance on the regime's maintenance. But the many horrendous economic and political outcomes (some of which have been pointed out here) leave an ever-present undercurrent of suspicion about the system's virtues.

It would be politically useful to shift the nature of the debate. It should become a debate about whether corporate capitalism *actually* delivers the good it promises and that this permits it to justify asking society to bear the occasional "malfunctioning" of the system. If this can be done, anti-capitalist activists might find themselves on a more favourable terrain of struggle. Pro–corporate capitalism advocates will have to show that the material wealth capitalists and their corporations produce outweighs the dysfunctionalities generated by their ceaseless drive for more. The uneven distribution of wealth and power, the many physical and psychic injuries inflicted by the chase for profits, the rending of the values and norms by which people other than capitalists believe they should live, all can be listed and elaborated to offset the satisfaction we are supposed to evince because, in the aggregate, monetary wealth is growing ever so nicely. Making this a focus of the attack on capitalists and their corporations can reveal that their reliance on the argument that "the most wickedest of men [doing] the wickedest of things" is a proper means to deliver the "bounty" of economic growth that we supposedly need and crave is inane, perhaps even insane. An argument that their calculation of wealth does not speak of a kind of wealth that meets the aspirations of human beings who want to live in a more altruistic, more compassionate, more ecologically nurturing society can be put on the agenda.

Changing the discourse and politics of anti-capitalists

The argument presented here aims at furthering this end. Its purpose is to change the terrain of struggle by eroding the resonance of claims that law allows us to express our autonomous wishes as we sell our labour power and that law is right not to allow any questioning of its assumptions as it is being applied to corporate activities. Once these challenges are issued, their strength will throw corporate capitalists onto the back foot. They will have to argue that exceptionalism for their wealth-creating activities is justified by the empirical results. I have endeavoured to show why and how it is possible to mount these challenges to the unwarranted privileging of corporate capitalism and provide tools so that anti-capitalist critics and activists can identify and reconfigure those features of the legal system that have been bastardized to serve corporate capitalism by casting it as a benign system that lives in harmony with our professed ideals. These are the tools:

- The characterization of corporations as sovereign individuals with their own agendas is not defensible and should be confronted constantly. Conceptually and materially, they are collectives endowed with disproportionate economic and political powers that benefit the contributors of capital to their coffers. Corporations are instruments designed to satisfy capitalists' drive for more. Their misbehaviours should be attributed to capitalism as a system and capitalists as people. Anti-capitalist activists and critics should not permit themselves to be distracted by legal proposals to reform corporations or by engaging with movements designed to persuade corporations to be more socially responsible. If, as argued here, capitalism is criminal *in nature*, it follows that, when they flout ethical and moral norms embedded in law or violate legally mandated standards, corporations are doing what comes naturally to red-blooded human capitalists and what they want their corporations to do. Given the frailty of the legal reasoning that bestows legal personality on an artificial being and that limits fiscal liability and removes legal responsibility from those who hide behind the novel legal person, anti-capitalist activists and critics would do well to argue for the abolition of corporations and hold their controllers' feet to the fire. An extended and cogent argument to this effect has been made by Steve Tombs and David Whyte in their recent work, *The Corporate Criminal*.[132]

- The effect of the establishment of regulatory laws as a special category of laws is to give likely harm-doers, capitalists and their corporations, a way to pretend that their conduct that offends our shared ethical and moral values or notions of the public interest are not offences at all. These are laws that give their blessing to a certain level of coerced taking and dispossession.[133] Anti-capitalist activists and critics might gain a great deal by demands that regulatees should not be allowed to participate in any way in setting the levels of harm they are to be permitted to inflict (as would-be thieves or robbers are not). They should insist that, whatever standards eventuate, violations should be seen as real crimes, that is, as behaviours that deserve the utmost condemnation and stigmatization. They should avoid the empty debates as to whether regulatory laws are real criminal laws or some other, not-so-serious, species of law.

- As corporations are given their agenda and character by those who use them to privately accumulate socially produced wealth, it is they, the sentient, individual capitalists, who should be targeted for the built-in risk-creation and risk-shifting that is the hallmark of corporate capitalism. In other work, I have compiled the data and made the argument that, although there are many kinds of investors in corporations, in most jurisdictions in the world (the exceptions being the U.S. and the U.K.), there are easily identifiable capitalists who control the bulk of corporations and who are in a position to set the agenda for the corporation and who give it its character.[134] By way of illustration, note that, in Australia, in 100 major listed corporations, 5 shareholders controlled 54 per cent of the shareholding; 10 controlled 64 per cent and 20 shareholders in these corporations controlled 70 per cent of the shares.[135] In short, a very few, easily identifiable people (contrast institutional investors) are beneficiaries and controllers of corporate conduct. In Canada, out of 247 publicly traded corporations, a mere 67 could be said to have diffuse ownership; the remainder had one to five shareholders in control of their shares and voting powers.[136] It is relatively easy to see which capitalists drive corporations (or blithely permit them) to behave as they do. The same is true in Hong Kong, India, Indonesia, Israel, Japan, Korea, Malaysia, The Philippines, Singapore, Taiwan, Thailand, Turkey, Argentine, Brazil, Chile, Columbia, Ecuador, Mexico, Peru, Austria, Belgium, Denmark, Finland, France, Germany, Greece, Iceland, Italy, The Netherlands, Norway, Portugal, Sweden, Switzerland … Even as the actual legal relations and duties and obligations in these jurisdictions differ, the degree of control by identifiable beneficiaries is very similar.[137] It is entirely feasible and makes eminent legal and moral sense to ensure that law, infused with liberal principles, should be made to hold flesh-and-blood driving capitalists hiding behind corporations responsible for the costs and injuries their corporations impose on others.

Let me restate the message being sent: the notion has been that law's philosophy of political and economic liberalism gives those who remain within its confines legitimacy. Capitalism and capitalists use law as a Trojan horse for their relentless pursuit for more. As Bertrand Russell has written:

> Advocates of capitalism are very apt to appeal to the sacred principles of liberty, which are embodied in the maxim: The for- · tunate must not be restrained in the exercise of tyranny over the unfortunate.[138]

Law, with its own need for legitimacy, cannot afford to be seen as being abused in this way. Yet it has yielded to capitalism's needs. It is impelled, first, to pretend that there are no distortions (though, as seen, it has to make gross assumptions about the voluntariness of employment contracts, the innocence of business planning and neutrality of risk-creation, and so on) and, second, that the distortions that become obvious (as in the treatment of violations of regulatory laws as, at worst, quasi-criminal) are of no great moment. This has allowed capitalists to carve out peculiar safe havens, self-standing islands of legal irresponsibility for themselves. Bringing out the frailties and illogicalities of the bending and tearing of the legal system will put capitalists and their corporations on the defensive. The hope is that this may help those of us who see ourselves as anti-capitalists, who are desirous to free ourselves from the fetters on our legal and political imaginations.

I Notes

1   *The Jungle: The Lost First Edition*, ed. Gene DeGruson (Memphis: St. Luke's Press, 1988), 83.

2   "On Institutional Stupidity," Issue 127, *Philosophy Now*, 4 April, 2015.

3   The data are grist for the daily grind of media mills. James Henry et al., of the Tax Justice Network, in their *Price of Offshore Revisited* (2012), report that somewhere between $21 trillion and $32 trillion sits in tax havens, contributing very little to government revenues. See also Gabriel Zucman, *The Hidden Wealth of Nations: The Scourge of Tax Havens*, rep'd ed. (Chicago: University of Chicago Press, 2016); Cass R. Sunstein, "Parking the Big Money," *New York Review of Books*, 14 Jan., 2016; Timothy McGrath, "The Top US Corporations Are Stashing $1.4 Trillion in Tax Havens," *Global Post*, 15 April, 2016. Because the corporations seek to hide their activities, the numbers compiled by various investigators differ, with Canadians for Tax Fairness telling a parliamentary committee that Canadians had dumped $160 billion in tax havens, depriving Canada of $7.8 billion in revenues, while *Huffington Post Canada*, 8 July, 2011, estimated that at least $270 billion had been diverted by Canadians to tax havens. Nassim Khadem and Craig Butt, "Which of Australia's Biggest Companies Are Not Paying Tax," *Sydney Morning Herald*, 17 Dec., 2015, report that the 1,539 companies in Australia with $100 million or more in annual turnover, amounting to $1.6 trillion in total, and $169.9 billion in profits, paid a combined $39.9 billion in taxes. An astonishing 38% of these companies paid no tax at all. Since these studies appeared, we have had the revelations of the Paradise Papers and the Panama Papers; before that it was the publication of the Luxembourg Leaks that gave life to the public anger about tax avoidance and tax evasion. These exposés were products of the work done by the International Consortium of Investigative Journalists.

4   N. Naffine, *The Law and the Sexes: Explorations in Feminist Jurisprudence* (Sydney: Allen & Unwin, 1990), 24.

5   With apologies to Ronald Dworkin (*Taking Rights Seriously* [Harvard University Press, 1978]) for this use of his terminology, which he, of course, used to establish the proposition that law is based on principles fundamental to all peoples. Here the argument is that this claim is one that is often disproved by facts on the ground.

6   2015 was the 800th anniversary of *Magna Carta*. Liberal legal and political philosophers joyfully celebrated it, even though it was enacted for non-liberal purposes. What makes it so useful to them is its recital of outright rejection of coercion exercised by the previously all-powerful monarchs: "No free man shall be seized or imprisoned or stripped of his rights or possessions or outlawed or exiled, or deprived of his standing in any other way, nor will we proceed with force against him, or send others to do so, except by lawful judgment of his equals or by the law of the land. To none will we sell, to no one deny or delay right or justice." This document's rejection of coercion of his subjects by a sovereign is what leads Anglo-American liberals to claim that their ideology (which celebrates the equal sovereignty of all individuals) has the weight of human history behind it.

7   D. Hay, "Time, Inequality, and Law's Violence," in Austin Sarat, ed., *Law's Violence* (Ann Arbor: University of Michigan Press, 1992). For a similar assessment, see Pierre Bourdieu, "The Force of Law: Toward a Sociology of the Juridical Field" (1987), 38 *Hastings L. Jo.* 839.

8   The literature doubting the utility of measuring welfare by national or gross domestic product metrics is vast. Here is a short and eclectic list: Herman Daly, "Dear Paul Krugman: Is GDP Growth Making Us Richer or Poorer?," *The Daly News*, 10 May, 2014; John McMurtry, "Breaking Out of the Invisible Prison: The Ten-Point Global Paradigm Revolution," *The Bullet*, 25 Feb., 2015; Elinor Ostrom, *Governing the Commons* (Cambridge University Press, 1991); R.H. Tawney, *The Acquisitive Society* (London/ Glasgow: Fontana Library, 1961, first pub. 1921); Coral Graham, *The Pursuit of Happiness: An Economy of Wellbeing* (Washington, DC.: Brookings Institute, 2011); Kent Greenfield, "New Principles for Corporate Law" [2005] *Hastings Business Law Jo.* 87.

9   A prestigious group of advocates who belong to the law and economics school pretend that there is no pretense. They contend that the corporate form is a mere convenience, that it is really just a way through which individual capitalists organize themselves as they pursue their individual profit-maximization goals. This is a school with much influence but, in the end, it fails to convince. Its scholars are forced to twist and turn as they seek to justify the limited liability and legal immunity that corporate law grants to these supposed sovereign and discrete contracting individuals. They are forced to claim that the corporation, that mere convenience, should be the person made legally responsible for the acts done on behalf of the free contracting individuals. The corporation, first ditched by these scholars, thus is brought back to life. This argument is based, rather feebly, not on principle but on assumptions that the markets will, somehow or other, push the responsibility imposed on the corporation onto the original contracting autonomous individuals. For my fuller critiques, see H. Glasbeek, "More Direct Directors Responsibility: Much Ado About … What?" (1995), 25 *Can. Bus. L. Jo.* 416; *Wealth by Stealth: Corporate Crime, Corporate Law, and the Perversion of Democracy* (Toronto: Between the Lines, 2002); *Class Privilege: How Law Shelters Shareholders and Coddles Capitalism* (Toronto: Between the Lines, 2017).

10   All that has to be done to register a corporation as a legal person is to convince a public administrator that the applicant is sane, not bankrupt, and over eighteen, and that the name to be given to the corporate firm is not already in use. It appears to be a readily available right. To form a union, not only does a registrar have discretion whether to register a union by assessing the applicant's compliance with a large number of qualifying requirements, but opponents of the applicant have a right to launch legal objections to such registration, making unionization more like a privilege than a right. For the hoops through which workers must jump to form a union in Canada, see Drache and Glasbeek, *The Changing Workplace: Reshaping Canada's Industrial Relations System* (James Lorimer, 1992); the position is broadly similar in the U.S. but slightly more restrictive as employers are given influence over the registration of unions process; for the position in Australia, see Andrew Stewart, Anthony Forsyth, Mark Irving, Richard Johnstone,

and Shae McCrystal, *Creighton & Stewart's Labour Law*, 6th ed. (Federation Press, 2016).

11   To legitimate the retention of a bargaining advantage for employers, the law implicitly relies on equating the investment made by an employee with an investment of private property by the employer. As will be seen shortly, this acknowledgement that what the employee invests is a form of property is abandoned when it comes to the characterization of the employment contract as a voluntary agreement between legal equals. If this *volte-face* was not done, it would become clear that the employment contract is the very obverse of a commercial contract and that to apply ordinary contract law principles to it makes no sense.

12   The right to withhold capital for any reason permits wealth owners to use this right as a political weapon, one used to gain economic advantage over workers. Even when workers are allowed to use collective power to bargain for terms of employment, they do not have the legal right to use this weapon politically, further enhancing the power of owners of wealth, while pretending that all is equal under law.

13   David Frank, *J.B. McLachlan: A Biography; The Story of a Legendary Labour Leader and the Cape Breton Coal Miners* (James Lorimer, 1999).

14   This trend is occasionally bucked, for example, Daumier's drawings, novels by Dickens, academic enfants terribles, but these critiques are overwhelmed by the popular cultural adorations of law and its processes.

15   This is not to say that all members of the public are convinced that the law is not biased toward the rich and powerful; see D. Gibson and J. Baldwin, eds., *Law in a Cynical Society?: Opinion and the Law in the 1980's* (Calgary/Vancouver: Carswell, 1985) for surveys that show that there is some scepticism. The Action Group on Access to Justice had such a survey done and it reported that 78% of Ontarians described the system as "old-fashioned," 71% as "intimidating," and more than 60% said it was "confusing," "inefficient," "broken." While this speaks to general dissatisfaction, rather than out-and-out bias, a main finding was that respondents believed that the rich got better access to justice than anyone else; for a more recent finding to this effect, see "Survey Finds Most Ontarians Say Justice System Is 'Broken,'" *Toronto Star*, 17 Oct., 2016, A1.

16   *63502 British Columbia Ltd.* v. *Minister of National Revenue* (1999),
248 N.R. 215 (Sup. Ct. Canada). In general, fines imposed for violations of
regulatory laws are deductible unless the violation is characterized as having
involved some kind of moral turpitude. The vagueness of this kind of criterion is pertinent to this section of this essay and useful to capitalists. The
Australian Institute of Directors objected to a proposal that directors should
be required to show that they attempted to prevent bribery as it was too
difficult to tell "legitimate relationship building activities, such as hospital-
ity" from bribery; see Nassim Khadem, "Australia a 'Soft Touch' for Foreign
Bribery, Inquiry Told," *WAToday*, 7 Aug., 2017. It suffices here to note that,
in line with the text that follows, there is an assumption that the mere fact
of a finding that the law was violated does not require us to see the violating
conduct as stigmatizable deviant behaviour, especially if it is associated with
that undoubted "good," a capitalist's endeavours to accumulate socially produced wealth for their private benefit. If fines or statutory penalties can be
labelled something else, say by having them paid to victims of the penalty-
attracting behaviour, they may become deductible as if they are income-
yielding expenditures; see Glasbeek, *Class Privilege*, 139ff.

17   Unsurprisingly, corporate actors justify their dubious incentive
schemes as forced on them by foreigners less sensible than "we" are to the
need not to gain unfair advantage. This helps explain why, in a series of
exposés of Australian bribery allegations, the researchers were able to list
apparently hapless blue-ribbon firms (BHP Billiton, Tenex, Lifese [Sydney
construction group], Leighton, Tabcorp, Sundance, Snowy Mountain
Engineering Group, Sinclair Knight Merz, Security/Note Printing
Australia, Thiess, Worley Parsons/Unaoil) of being involved in suspicious
activities; see McKenzie, Freudenthal, Bachelard, and Baker, "Australian
Companies Linked to Bribe Scandals in Sri Lanka and Congo," *WAToday*,
25 Aug., 2016.

18   *McDonnell* v. *United States*, No. 15-174, 27 June, 2016 (Sup. Ct. US). A
study done for the Institute of New Economic Thinking by London Business
School researchers Ahmed Tahoun and Florin Vasvari found that members
of U.S. Senate and House of Representatives finance committees consistently
got loans with more generous terms than other legislators and that they took

out more and greater loans. It might be difficult in law to hold that legislators act improperly when accepting such favourable terms, but it is not difficult to see that they might be in breach of the spirit of the ethics and protocols that guide their professional lives; see David Sirota, "Lawmakers Overseeing Wall Street Given Bigger, More Favorable Loans Than Others: Study," *International Business Times*, 20 Aug., 2016.

19   *Citizens United* v. *Federal Electoral Commission* (2010), 558 U.S. 310 (Sup. Ct. US).

20   *U.S.A.* v. *Weimert*, US District Ct for Western District of Wisconsin, No. 15-2453, (April 8, 2016).

21   *C.F.R. Holdings Ltd.* v. *Fundy Chemical International Ltd.* (1980), 14 C.C.L.T. 87 (B.C.). This carefree attitude to commercial dishonesty is common; see Canadian Press, 10 March, 2017, "Justin Trudeau Defends Bombardier Loan Despite Bribery Charges against Official in Sweden," quoting Michael Nadeau, Director of the Institute for Governance of Private and Public Corporations: "It is part of the daily life of big corporations that do business with governments … to be accused of corruption."

22   For a misleading advertising prosecution to succeed, it must be proved beyond a reasonable doubt that the targeted consumers would have relied on the statements as material (note that slippery word again) to their decision to purchase the product or service. This is exceptionally difficult. As Daniel J. Boorstin, *The Image: A Guide to Pseudo Events in America* (Vintage, 1992) found, we have come to live in world of half-truths, in a thicket of unreality. In this world, most advertising is portrayed by law as harmless tomfoolery that everyone recognizes for what it is. This raises the question: Why would profit-maximizing and cost-cutting capitalists spend so much money on communications that are largely disregarded by the recipients? Moreover, it ignores the fact that advertising saturation not only promotes ugly and dangerous stereotyping but also does much to convert citizenship into consumerism, something of inestimable value to corporate capitalists. See Naomi Klein, *No Logo*, 10th anniversary ed. (Picador, 2009); Joel Bakan, *Childhood under Siege: How Big Business Targets Your Children* (Free Press, 2102); Gerbner and Gross, "Living with Television: The Violence Profile," *Jo. of Communications*, Spring, 1976, observing that "a common consciousness

is being created by the bombardment of marketing messages ... an encul-
turation with the impact of religious teachings."

23 See Harry Glasbeek, "Enron and Its Aftermath: Can Reforms
Restore Confidence?," in Anand, Connidis, and Flanagan, eds., *Crime in
the Corporation* (Queen's Annual Business Law Symposium, 2004). In this
essay, the focus is on the way in which judges and lawyers have granted
themselves the freedom to pursue political and social biases to favour capitalism writ large while purporting to follow the dictates of law. This same
liberty is not just used to favour corporate capitalists; it also allows judges to
pursue their predilections for social outcomes they personally favour while
pretending to adhere to fundamental principles. To take but one example:
there is a legal doctrine, known as the Rule in *Rylands* v. *Fletcher*, that makes
any person who allows something unnatural on his land to escape, which
then causes harm to another, strictly liable for that harm. When a cricket
ball was hit over a fence, hitting a pedestrian, the rule of strict liability for
the harm done by an escape of something not naturally on land was ditched.
Neither a legal nor a policy reason was given for this contemptuous jetti-
soning of an ancient principle. A short paragraph stating the conclusion,
that the principle was inapplicable, was all that was offered. The unstated
reasoning was easy to divine but too embarrassing to articulate. It was that
cricket is much beloved by English judges and was not to be inhibited by the
strict application of a well-known letter of the law; see *Bolton* v. *Stone*, [1951]
A.C. 850 (House of Lords).

24 The shippers' association case was *Mogul Steamship Co.* v. *McGregor,
Gow & Co.*, [1892] A.C. 25 and the cited passage is from Lord Halsbury's
speech; see pp. 36–7. For the dramatically contrasting approach when it came
to union solidarity, see *Quinn* v. *Leathem*, [1909] A. C. 495. It was not until
the decisions in *McKernan* v. *Fraser* (1931), 46 C.L.R. 343 and *Crofter Hand
Woven Harris Tweed Co. Ltd.* v. *Veitch*, [1942] A.C. 435, that the Australian
and English courts, much criticized for their obvious preference for entrepreneurs over workers and confronted by legislative and political realities
that endowed trade unions with greater legal standing, permitted workers
to pursue their own interests with more economic vigour. This well-trodden
history of apparent judicial bias when applying supposedly liberal law drew

much critical commentary; see E.I. Sykes, *Strike Law in Australia*, 2nd ed. (Sydney: Law Book Co.); J.H. Portus, *The Development of Australian Trade Union Law* (Carlton: Melbourne University Press, 1958); Hickling, *Citrine's Trade Union Law,* 3rd ed. (London: Stevens & Sons, 1967); Innis M. Christie, *The Liability of Strikers in the Law of Tort: A Comparative Study of the Law in England and Canada* (Kingston, ON: Queen's University, Industrial Relations Centre, 1967); Judy Fudge and Eric Tucker, *Labour before the Law: Collective Action in Canada, 1900–1948* (Toronto: Oxford University Press, 2001); W. Wedderburn, *The Worker and the Law*, 3rd ed. (Harmondsworth: Penguin Books, 1986). It led to legislative alleviations, but they were never generous enough to free worker collective action from judicial fetters imposed on behalf of capitalists regardless of how much this offended the spirit of liberal law's claim to evenhandedness. Examples are provided in the brief notes on the torts of inducing breach of contract and intimidation that follow in the text. For another illustration of how economic coercion of workers is tolerable to the common law mind, note *Matthew* v. *Bobbins*, [1980] Property & Conveyancing Rep. 1, where the very judge who pioneered the idea that some contracts should be set aside when the difference in bargaining power made it an unconscionable agreement held that this doctrine should never apply to employer-employee relations.

25   All market economies have enacted pro-competition, anti-combines legislation.

26   This is another instance of the utility of the law and economics school to the corporate world. Its claim that the corporation is really just a shell and that the combination is just a nexus of contracts between individual shareholders, creditors, workers, and the like, negates the notion that there is a separate entity, a collective that presents the usual problems that all combinations present to our idealized system. But of course, that school's equal support for the lack of personal responsibility of the self-same individual contractors when something goes wrong does undermine its otherwise clever riposte. The corporation, as a functional collective entity, has more coercive power than would the individual contributors to its coffers. This always threatens to undermine the claim that its existence and modes of operation dovetail with the tenets of a liberal philosophy and market economics.

27   It is true that, in some very few cases, courts will remove the corporate veil and hold those who hide behind it responsible for conduct engaged in via the corporate person. But the very exceptionalism of the piercing of the veil weaponry only serves to confirm the idea that a corporation is ordinarily a real person, separate from all other persons; see H. Glasbeek, "Preliminary Observations on Strains of, and Strains in, Corporate Law Scholarship," in F. Pearce and L. Snider, eds., *Corporate Crime: Contemporary Debates* (Toronto: University of Toronto Press, 1995), 111.

28   See n. 8 above and accompanying text for doubts about the utility of growth promoted by means of corporate capitalism.

29   This concern that property owners should not have to pay up front lest their profit-seeking activities be impaired has a flip side. The same property owners refuse to pay workers up front for their work. Workers are paid in arrears: this allows employers to claim, as their property, the product of their workers and it acts as a disciplinary weapon that helps ensure that workers meet their obligations. Tax gatherers are not to be so favoured when they confront corporate actors who might well want to avoid *their* obligations.

30   Law Reform Commission of Canada, *Our Criminal Law* (Ottawa: Information Canada, 1976); see also Rutland et al., eds., *James Madison, 14: The Papers of James Madison* (1983), citing Madison's writing in 1792: "Government is instituted to protect property of every sort…. This being the end of government, that alone is a *just* government, which *impartially* secures to every man, whatever is his *own*"; see also Cox et al., eds., *John Locke, Second Treatise of Government* (1983), at p. 75: "The great and chief end therefore, of men's uniting into commonwealths, and putting themselves under government, is the preservation of *property*."

31   See *R. v. Mckinlay Transport Ltd*, [1990] 1 S.C.R. 627 (Sup. Ct. Canada). A similar sentiment moved the then Chief Justice of the High Court of Australia to render s. 260 of the Australian revenue statute (whose purpose is to prevent evasion of taxation by criminalizing it) toothless; see Geoffrey Lehman, "The Income Tax Judgments of Sir Garfield Barwick: A Study in the Failure of New Legalism" (1983), 9 *Melb. Uni. L.R.* 115; David Marr, *Barwick* (Allen & Unwin, 1980). Such assumptions support the proposition that tax minimizers are pursuing a virtuous path. It is both moral

and sensible to dilute the power of the state to take away property owned by private wealth owners. As will be seen below, similar assumptions make it difficult to regulate entrepreneurial activity in any meaningful manner.

32 Kimiko De Freytas-Tamura, "Welsh Town Leads a British Revolt against the Tax System and Corporations," *New York Times*, 21 Feb., 2016, captures the anger of a local citizenry. Here are some quotes collected by the reporter: "'It's just wrong,'" said Steven Askew, a baker in Crickhowell.... He and his wife ... paid more income tax than Facebook. 'Someone's got to stand up and say enough is enough. Enough with the injustice,' he added.... Rose Tabb ... was adamant. 'Either we all pay, or we don't.'"

33 (1981), 35 N.R. 451 (Sup. Ct. Canada).

34 Nils Christie, *A Sustainable Amount of Crime* (Psychology Press, 2004), 7.

35 [1931] A.C. 310, p. 324 (Privy Council).

36 As noted earlier, these processes are integral to the imposition of fetters on the state's otherwise legitimated use of coercive powers. Most important among these fetters is that the state should be wary of criminalizing conduct without good reason; see Law Reform Commission of Canada, *Our Criminal Law*, n. 30. Coercion is seen as an evil. This is the core of this essay: if law is manipulated to allow or promote coercion, it is being bent out of shape.

37 Lord Devlin, *The Enforcement of Morals* (Oxford University Press, 1965). The colourful language (indignation, disgust, intolerance) likely was due to the context, a discussion of England's laws prohibiting sexual relations between consulting male adults. Devlin wrote his account in 1959 (publ. 1965) and it became, and remains, a standard defence of liberal moralism as a basis for criminalizing conduct. The vagueness of his formulation led to an immediate and vinegary reply by H.L.A. Hart, "Immorality and Treason," *Listener* 62; see also his *Law, Liberty and Morality* (Vintage Books, 1963).

38 Francis Allen, *Borderland of Criminal Justice: Essays in Law and Criminology* (Chicago: University of Chicago Press, 1964).

39 G. Williams, *Textbook on Criminal Law* (London: Stevens, 1983), 936.

40 The literature is voluminous. To make my few observations, I consulted Dworkin, Devlin, Hart, Williams, and the Law Reform Commission

of Canada, all cited above, as well as J.S. Mill, *On Liberty*, Gateway Edition;
G. Fletcher, *Basic Concepts of Criminal Law* (Oxford University Press, 1998);
L. Alexander, *Crime and Culpability: A Theory of Criminal Law* (Cambridge
University Press, 2009); Michael Moore, *Placing Blame: A Theory of the
Criminal Law* (Oxford University Press, 2010); A. Norrie, *Crime, Reason
and History: A Critical Introduction to Criminal Law*, 3rd ed. (Cambridge
University Press, 2014); J. Abell and E. Sheehy, *Criminal Law and Procedure:
Cases, Context, Critique*, 3rd ed. (Captus Press, 2002); S. Bronitt and B.
McSherry, *Principles of Criminal Law* (Thomson Reuter, 2010).

41 P. Sweezy, *The Theory of Capitalist Development: Principles of
Marxian Political Economy* (New York: Monthly Review Press, 1942), 56:
"[u]nder capitalism ownership of the means of production is vested with
one set of individuals while work is performed by another—the buying and
selling of labour power is the differentia specifica of capitalism."

42 The reappearance of wide disparities in wealth is undisputed.
Oxfam reports that, in 2015, 62 individuals owned as much wealth as the
poorest 3.6 billion people in the world. The Credit Suisse Research Institute's
Global Wealth Report, 28 Dec., 2016, reports that three-quarters of the global
adult population, i.e., 3.5 billion people, had assets worth less than $10,000,
in aggregate accounting for 2.4% of global wealth; billionaires, comprising
less than 1% of total population, owned 46% of global wealth. In Canada,
David Macdonald, "Outrageous Fortune: Documenting Canada's Wealth
Gap" (Canadian Centre for Policy Alternatives, April 2014) records that 86
people, that is, 0.002% of the population, had more wealth than the poorest 11.4 million Canadians; the bottom 20% of families had more debt than
assets. In Australia, Oxfam showed that, in 2015, the top 1% of wealth owners
owned as much wealth as the poorest 60% of the population. For longer and
more nuanced accounts, see T. Piketty, *Capital in the Twenty-First Century*,
tr. Arthur Goldhammer (Cambridge/London: Belknap Press, 2014);
Anthony B. Atkinson, *Inequality: What Can Be Done?* (Harvard University
Press, 2015); Joseph E. Stiglitz, *The Price of Inequality: How Today's Divided
Society Endangers Our Future* (W.W. Norton, 2013); R. Wilkinson and K.
Pickell, *The Spirit Level*, rep. ed. (Bloomsbury Press, 2011).

43   R.L. Fischl, "Some Realism about Critical Legal Studies" (1987), 41 *Uni. Miami L. Rev.* 505, 527–8, relates that, when he asks students to find a rationale for allowing the employer to retain the workers' product, the students eventually have to admit that, if it were otherwise, that is, if the employer could not expropriate the wealth socially produced by its workers, there would be no capitalism. Stephen A. Margolin, (1974), 6 *Review of Radical Political Economics* 60, 112, provides a historical and theoretical overview of how capitalists revamped modes of production to enable them to appropriate surplus value created by workers. That is, what is now intuitively understood to be the norm had to be fought for and won by capitalists.

44   See A. Leff, "Unconscionability and the Code—The Emperor's New Clothes" (1967), 15 *Uni. Penn. L. Rev.* 485, for this colourful way of pointing out that voluntariness is sacred. Coercion can take many forms and Leff is saying that, when it is found to exist, a contract becomes unenforceable. This suggests that there might be such a thing as a non-coercive contract. For the purposes of the argument in this essay, this is not quibbled about here, but it is a dubious proposition. When the Realist school of jurisprudence held sway in legal circles, scholars contended that the essence of any contract was coercion because it always involved a threat of adverse consequences unless an agreement was concluded on certain terms. Basic to this understanding was the belief that coercion was the essence of economic life under a capitalist system, a far cry from the dominant contemporary idea that contracts, markets, and trade can be "free." See Robert Hale, "Bargaining, Duress and Economic Liberty" (1943), 43 *Col. Law. Rev.* 605; *Freedom through Law: Public Control of Private Power* (New York: Columbia University Press, 1952); Morris Cohen, "The Basis of Contract" (1933), 46 *Harv. L. Rev.* 553; B. Mensch, "Freedom of Contract as Ideology" (1981), 33 *Stanford Law. Rev.* 753. For an overview, see Kerry Rittich, *Recharacterizing Restructuring* (The Hague/London/New York: Kluwer International, 2002). In this essay, the special case of employment contracts has been selected to dramatize the point about inherent coercion because, in this setting, there is easily visible coercion (at least to anyone who cares to look). It is so blatant that it should be anathema to anyone who adheres to a liberal polity's values.

45 O. Kahn-Freund, *Labour and the Law*, 2nd ed. (London: Stevens &
Sons, 1972), 2–8; see also Mark Irving, *The Contract of Employment* (Sydney:
LexisNexis, 2012), stating that the duty to obey is "one of the identifying
features of employment," it being "coterminous with the contract" (350–51).

46 Report of the Task Force on Labour Relations (the Woods Task
Force), *Canadian Industrial Relations* (Ottawa: Privy Council, 1968), para.
291. The task force went on to support collective bargaining as its preferred
mechanism of adjustment to deal with capital/labour relations. But it felt
it necessary to acknowledge that the "underlying concepts of the free individual, private property and freedom of contract" provided the enduring
platform for the capitalist "mixed economy" it favoured (para. 30). That is,
it proposed a conditions and terms modifying collective bargaining scheme
to be built on top of the contract of employment, not one that replaced its
essential concepts.

47 H. Glasbeek, "Labour Relations' Policy and Law as a Mechanism of
Adjustment" (1987), 25 *Osgoode Hall Law Journal*, 179; "The Utility of Model
Building: Collins' Capitalist Discipline and Corporatist Law" (1984), 12 *Ind.
L. Jo.* 133. It is passing strange, if all this is acknowledged, that scholars and
policy-makers hang onto the argument that work-for-wages contracts may
be read as agreements between equally sovereign individuals and that it
makes sense to hold that workers *voluntarily* agree to the employer's taking
of their product.

48 Gabrielle Goldring, "Terms Implied by Law into Employment
Contracts: Are They Necessary?" (2015), 28 *Aust. Jo. Labour Law* 113, argues
for a rationale that will aid courts that strive for justice and better policy
(acknowledging that, in the absence of such terms, justice and good policy
will be scarce) when implying terms into employment contracts. The argument is that there is something special about work-for-wages contracts (they
are "relational," "co-operative," code words to deal with the unmentionable
and disagreeable facts, namely, the reality about what is being bought and sold
for what purpose) that needs to be recognized. It may require legal support
for its viability as a distinct arrangement. But the author, urging courts to be
benign as they acknowledge the need to perfect this special relationship, starts
off by saying that some minimal terms *must* remain part of every contract

of employment, in particular, "the duty for an employee to obey lawful instructions could also be considered necessary" to facilitate "the employer's capacity to manage its work force." Co-operation and long-term relations, suggesting trust and equality between the parties, are to be backed up by granting legal force to one of the parties to make the other do what it wants.

49 The title of Milton Friedman's work is tell-tale: *Capitalism and Freedom* (Chicago: University of Chicago Press, 1962). The critique is found in C.B. Macpherson, "Elegant Tombstones: A Note on Friedman's Freedom," *Canadian Journal of Political Science*, 1, 8 (1968).

50 *Federated Engine-Drivers and Firemen's Association of Australia* v. *The Broken Hill Propriety Company Ltd.* (1911), 5 C.A.R. 12. Equally colourfully, if more pretentiously, Farwell, L.J., had commented on the built-in imbalance in economic bargaining power in England in his decision in *Devonald* v. *Rosser*, [1906] 2 K.B. 728. At p. 743, he noted that workers live *de die in diem* because wages do not leave any scope for saving for a future day when no employment is available, whereas employers are in a position to plan their living over the long haul because profits are "ascertained, as an ordinary rule, *de anno in annum.*"

51 A.H. Ruegg, *The Law Regulating the Relations of Employers and Workmen in England* (London: W.W. Clowes, 1905). While there is no space to elaborate the issue, it is pertinent to note that one of the forms of workers' resistance to the new capitalist modes of production took the form of pilfering of materials employers had to entrust to workers. The workers claimed entitlement to such "extras" on the bases of custom and tradition. P. Linebaugh, *The London Hanged: Crime and Civil Society in the 18th Century* (London: Verso, 1991) argues that this gave a new direction to policing. Rather than being part of the overall administration of the state welfare system, there was a new emphasis aimed at assisting developing capitalist relations of production. Linebaugh's contention is that the police task was to impose the wage labour relation as the dominant workplace relationship. Workers and criminals were identified as overlapping groups, laying a basis for class differentiation. One class, the non-pilfering/work-for-wages class, was seen as distinct from the other. Linebaugh's take identifies this new kind of policing as a major tool in the creation and maintenance of class

relations. For echoing views, see Todd Gordon, *Cops, Crime and Capitalism: The Law and Order Agenda in Canada* (Halifax: Fernwood, 2006); Mark Neocleous, *Administering Civil Society: Toward a Theory of State Power* (London: Palgrave Macmillan, 1996); Lesley J. Wood, *Crisis and Control: The Militarization of Protest and Policing* (London/Toronto: Pluto Press, Between the Lines, 2014). Note how this protection of capitalists' private property from pilfering dovetails with the modern identification by the Law Reform Commission of Canada of theft as the paradigmatic crime. As will be noted below, workers also pushed for the franchise where they hoped their numbers could be used to restrain the power of the wealthy few and, of course, they tried to form trade unions in order to stop employers from causing them to compete with each other for scarce jobs.

52 *Davies* v. *Davies* (1887), 36 Ch. D. 359, 93. The contemporary, not directly enforceable, Universal Declaration of Human Rights echoes this nineteenth-century principle.

53 There is an exception in this U.S. constitutional protection: servitude is permitted if it is intended as a punishment for a convicted criminal. This goes some way to support the argument made in this paper that there is an agreement that coercion is wrong in principle and always needs justification. The legal trick, therefore, is to cast some coercive practices as noncoercive, here some employment contractual coercions as not constituting incidents of servitude. The text asks whether this legal trickery stands up when measured against our supposedly shared values and norms.

54 For an overview of the servility of workers under that pre-existing system and then its transposition to the new era of free contracting, see D. Hay and P. Craven, eds., *Masters, Servants and Magistrates in Britain and the Empire, 1562–1955* (University of Northern Carolina Press, 2004).

55 For the argument that the movement from status to contract, from a society where one's conditions of life depended on one's status rather than on one's abilities and endeavours, was widely seen as a sign of social progress; see Henry Maine, *Ancient Laws: Its Connection with Early History of Society, and Its Relation to Modern Ideas* (London: John Murray, 1861).

56 The tort is often known as the tort in *Lumley* v. *Gye*, (1853), 118 E.R. 749, the action in which it was decided that what formerly had been a crime

when it involved lowly servants could be the basis for a civil action involving even high-status employees. This tortious action, not so incidentally given the nature of the argument in this essay, gives employers additional power over collectivized workers. Most importantly, it allows employers to seek injunctive relief against trade unions asking workers to take industrial action, that is, to refuse to fulfill their contractual obligations. Inevitably, trade unions have had to seek legislative protections against this judicially created fetter on their powers. They succeeded quite early in the U.K. and Canada, and later in Australia. But, as recent Australian experience shows, employers continually seek to reassert their right to revive the common law action.

57   [1964] 1 All E.R. 367 (HL).

58   Liberalism posits that a society's nature should be the outcome of processes engaged in by all its interacting autonomous members. There is no blueprint as we are all different, each of us entitled to our own view of what is good and bad. Conceptually, liberal philosophy rejects the notion that there should be a preferred societal design; a planned society is counterintuitive to it. This is why it opposes the idea and ideals of a planned society. To modern liberals, the market is a process to be privileged because it leaves it to sovereign individuals to satisfy their self-identified, non-utopian, needs and wants.

59   Oscar Wilde, *The Soul of Man under Socialism* (London/New York: Journeyman Chapbook, rep'd 1988, first published 1891).

60   On the U.K., see Paul Smith, "Labour under the Law: A New Law of Combination, and Master and Servant, in 21st-Century Britain?" (2015), 46 *Ind. Rel. Jo.*, 345; on Canada, see Eric Tucker, "Shall Wagnerianism Have No Dominium?" *Osgoode Legal Studies Research Paper 49*, 2014; the vanishing protections in the U.S. are notorious (see Kate Andras, "The New Labor Law" (2016), 126 *Yale Law Jo.* 5); and, in Australia, the attacks by means of the Work Choices legislation, the fights over its repeal, and the potential for some of its more pernicious features' revival are central to current electoral politics.

61   The astonishing resonance of the tag "We are the 99%" is, in large part, explained by the glaring imbalance in wealth and power leading to

the satisfaction of the (very) few and the coercion of the many; see also Guy
Standing, *The Precariat: The New Dangerous Class*, reprint ed. (Bloomsbury
Academic, 2014). The word "precariat" in the title is derived from the word
"precarious" that, in turn, finds its origin in the Latin word "precarius," sig-
nifying, among other things, "prayer," "entreating another person." These are
survival methods that need to be used only by people who are a pale imitation
of idealized sovereign, autonomous individuals. Benjamin Selway, "Global
Value Chains or Global Poverty Chains: A New Research Agenda," CGPE
(Centre for Global Political Economy) Working Paper, no. 10, 2016, records
that, conservatively, one in three of the world's workforce earns less than two
dollars per day, the International Labour Organization's official measure of
poverty wages. Often it is major multinationals that seek to profit from this
kind of economic exploitation; see, for example, "Coca-Cola Manufacturer
Accused of Using Slave Labor in Brazil," *teleSUR*, 26 Aug., 2016. The reference to slavery in the title of that article might be legally incorrect but the
evidence offered reveals extreme oppression of workers, making their conditions more like servile incidents than acceptable contractual terms. Even
in the more mature capitalist countries, it is easy to find gross instances of
exploitation; see Chris Drisdale, "Foreign Workers Being Exploited to Grow
Pot," *Toronto Star*, 14 Aug., 2017, A11, noting that migrant visa labourers are
used in agriculture. They are issued a closed permit. This means they can only
work for one employer and, fearing deportation, are subject to its whims. In
Ontario, a report to the government, *Changing Workplaces Review*, reported
a huge number of cases in which employees were paid less than the statutory
minimum, denied statutorily required overtime, to the estimated tune of $28
million (as reported in *Toronto Star*, 2 Aug., 2016); this kind of wage theft
is also reported in the U.S., where the study in three cities in 2008, *Broken
Laws, Unprotected Workers*, found that an extrapolation from those data
meant that wage theft might amount to $20 billion per annum; see Jeff Spross,
"America's Hidden Crime Wave: Employers Steal $20 Billion from American
Workers Every Year," *The Week*, 17 Aug., 2016. For the normality of it all in
the U.S. and Canada, see Laureen Snider, "How Do I Discipline Thee: Let Me
Count the Ways *or* Tightening the Screws on the 99%," Osgoode Hall Law
School, Workshop, *Law and Class*, 28 June, 2017. Recent exposés in Australia

(Adele Ferguson, Sarah Danckert, and Klaus Toft, "7-Eleven: Investigation Exposes Shocking Exploitation of Convenience Store Workers," *The Age*, 30 Aug., 2015; Ben Schneiders and Royce Millar, "'Black Jobs': Rampant Exploitation of Foreign Workers in Australia Revealed", *WAToday*, 1 Oct., 2105; Ben Schneiders and Royce Millar, "Coles Knew More Than Half of Its Workers Were Underpaid," *SMH*, 20 Aug., 2016), speak to gross underpayment in violation of laws. Precarious work is not merely an occasional companion to corporate capitalism. Capitalists exercise their coercive powers and they do so systematically.

62   David Whyte, "Naked Labour: Putting Agamben to Work" (2009), 31 *Aust. Feminist L. Jo.* 52.

63   David Korten, "Buccaneers to Profiteers: On the Origin of Corporations," *YES! Magazine*, 8 March, 2011.

64   Robert Myles, *Capitalism and Unfree Labour: Anomaly or Exception?* (London: Tavistock, 1987), 86. The notion that workers should be forced into selling their labour cheaply was not confined to the colonies. Mandeville, *The Fable of the Bees* (1714, F. Kaye ed., 1924), at 193–4, advocated that "great numbers should be wretched as well as poor.... The poor have nothing to stir them up to be serviceable but their wants, which is prudence to relieve, but folly to cure ... they ought to be kept from starving ... they should receive nothing worth saving." Arthur Young, *Eastern Tour* 1771, Vol. IV, 361, summed it up: "Everyone but an idiot knows that the lower classes must be kept poor, or they will never be industrious."

65   There is no space to expand this argument, but it should be noted that many of the objections to free trade agreements, such as the Agreement on Trade-Related Aspects of Intellectual Property Rights (TRIPS) and the Trans-Pacific Partnership Agreement (TPPA), are that these deals will allow private multinational corporations to challenge otherwise autonomous governments' decisions that affect the property rights of these corporations and that they will be entitled to do so in fora not controlled by those governments; see Chris Hamby, "The Secret Court That Allows Corporations to Avoid Punishment for Enormous Crimes," *BuzzFeed*, 1 Sept., 2016. Electoral democratic institutions are marginalized as the transnational corporations, like the colonizing companies of yore, bring their entitlements obtained

under foreign laws with them. The U.S. has withdrawn from the TPPA nego-
tiations but the deal is not dead and there are many other similar deals on
the books.

66   What is not being argued is that these workers have entered into
these terrible arrangements unknowingly. They must be accorded respect;
they have agency. What is being argued is that the choices they have are
so limited that their agency is so circumscribed as to become miniscule. If
these kinds of contracts are treated as worthy of legal protection because of
their "voluntariness," the concept of voluntarism becomes a hollow one. The
gap between de jure and de facto autonomy is a gaping chasm.

67   B.R. Ambedkar, *Annihilation of Caste: The Annotated Edition* (New
Dehli: Navayana Publishing, 2014), 261.

68   The scholarly literature and the reports on the state of international
human rights law constitute a huge dossier. There is much controversy about
the scope and efficacy of the institutions and laws spawned. At their core,
focused as they are on the protection of individuals, they fit neatly into liberal law's positioning of the individual at the centre of its project. It follows
that they are well-suited tools when it is desired to name, blame, and shame
a practice that leads to discrimination against, coercion of, or physical harm
to an individual. But it is difficult to enforce claims that arise from labelling
a practice to be a human rights violation. There are definitional and scope
problems, particularly the question as to whether human rights laws should
apply to the repression of collective and economic rights. This has led to
vigorous debates in labour relations law circles (the sphere on which the text
is concentrating at this point). See Roy J. Adams, *Labor Left Out: Canada's
Failure to Protect and Promote Collective Bargaining as a Human Right*
(CCPA, 2005); Larry Savage, "Labour Rights as Human Rights? A Response
to Roy Adams," *Just Labour: A Canadian Journal of Work & Society*, vol.
12, Spring, 2008, 68; Lance Compa, "Labor's New Opening to International
Human Rights Standards," *Working USA: The Journal of Labor and Society
1*, March 2009, 98, 116; Jay Youngdahl, "Solidarity First—Labor Rights Are
Not the Same as Human Rights," Lance Compa, "Solidarity *and* Human
Rights—A Response to Youngdahl" in "Should Labor Defend Worker Rights
as Human Rights? A Debate," *New Labour Forum* 18 (10, 31, Winter 2009);

Nelson Lichtenstein, "The Rights Revolution," *New Labor Forum* 12–1, 2003, 68; T. Campbell and K. Ewing, eds., *The Legal Protection of Human Rights: Sceptical Essays* (Oxford: Oxford University Press, 2011); Keith Ewing and J. Hendy, QC, "The Trade Union Act 2016 and the Failure of Human Rights" (2016), 45 *Industrial Law Jo.*, 391. Another difficulty is that, often, the alleged violation of human rights is a permitted act in the jurisdiction where it occurs, even if it offends the human rights regime of the jurisdiction that the profit-seeking corporation uses as its home base. Further, it is legally and politically difficult to have the international standards enforced; see Kenneth Roth, "Defending Economic, Social and Cultural Rights: Practical Issues Faced by an International Human Rights Organization," *Human Rights Quarterly* 26, 2004, 63. There has been a recent spate of actions against corporations in Canada on the basis that their subsidiaries and contractors and the relevant foreign government have abused human rights on their behalf. Although these actions are couched in the language of human rights violations, the claims made are typically civil law ones, asking for compensation for physical, environmental, and cultural harms. The success rate is low and it takes eons to complete such actions. They do, however, serve a symbolic, educational purpose. For the purposes of this paper, this is important: the lesson being taught is that otherwise legal profit-seeking may be so offensive that it should be thought of as criminal in nature, even if it is extremely difficult to call it criminal in the strict legal meaning of that term and it leads to claims for compensation from, rather than punishment of, the wrongdoers. Not only is restitution sought, but such actions are cathartic because they may do much—as a normal criminal prosecution might—to stigmatize the defendant and the kind of practices from which it sought to profit.

69   D. Vogel, *The Market for Virtue: The Potential and Limits of Corporate Social Responsibility* (Washington: Brookings Institution, 2005), recorded that Wal-Mart had 100,000 and Disney 30,000 suppliers vying for their business; see also C. Fishman, "The Wal-Mart You Don't Know," *Fast Company*, Issue 77, 2003, 68, and Harry Glasbeek, "Looking for Responsibility in the Corporate World *or* The Corporation's Multiple Personality Disorder," in Helen Anderson, ed., *Directors' Personal Liability for Corporate Fault: A Comparative Analysis* (Wolters Kluwer, 2008).

70   A report by the *International Labor Rights Forum*, 9 March, 2016, "Uzbek and Global Activists Petition World Bank President to Suspend Payments," details efforts to put pressure on government-sponsored policy to use child labour in the cotton fields. Here are increasing reports demonstrating that modern, like old, capitalism lives happily with child exploitation and (see n. 71) slavery; see Josh Jacobs and Reeva Misra, "Child Labour Changing, Not Vanishing," *Washington Post*, 2 Sept., 2017, IN9, commenting on a report by Save the Children India that claims that 33 million children from ages 5 to 18 are working, despite laws forbidding such practices.

71   Carl Gibson, "How the iPhone6 Helps Perpetuate Modern-Day Slavery," *Reader Supported News*, 10 Sept., 2014. A bill proposed in Australia, arguing that there are at least 4,500 people trapped in slavery in that country, will require corporations with an annual turnover of $100 million to provide a statement every year on how they combat slavery at home and in their overseas ventures. While the term slavery is used somewhat loosely, this is an acknowledgement that millions of people work under conditions with too many servile incidents to be called voluntary employees. The United Nations' 2016 *Global Slavery Index* estimates there are 45.8 million people who can be classified as slave labourers. The British have enacted a *Modern Slavery Act*. In the U.S., the Southern Poverty Law Center's 2013 report, *Close to Slavery: Guestworker Programs in the United States*, provides more grim evidence of the determined efforts of capitalists to exploit workers.

72   In Europe, there was the *Accord on Fire and Building Safety in Bangladesh*; in the U.S., the *Bangladesh Worker Safety Initiative*. For an appraisal, see Beryl terHaar and Maarten Keune, "One Step Forward or More Window Dressing? A Legal Analysis of Recent CSR Initiatives in the Garment Industry in Bangladesh" [2014] *Int. Jo. Comp. Law*, 5. For a pessimistic account, see Elizabeth Winkler, "How Fair Labour Buzzwords Can Obscure the Truth," *Toronto Star*, 26 Aug., 2017; for a call to do better, see Lynda Yanz and Barry Fowler, "Cambodia's Abandoned Garment Workers Deserve Justice," *Toronto Star*, 24 June, 2017. For a recent illustration of how strong the push for exploitation remains, even as corporate actors evince their intention to be socially responsible capitalists, see Caitrin McKee, "Honduran Women Farm Workers Are Fighting Back Against Fyffes

Company's Abuses," *International Labor Rights Forum*, 7 March, 2017, detailing how an Irish company's supplier in Honduras allegedly had exposed its melon gathering workforce to poisonous materials, and paid them less than the minimum wage. Fyffes claimed it would look into all these allegations, even as it turns out that there are other, similar, allegations against it and its suppliers. Fyffes is a member of Ethical Trading Initiative that demands its members adhere to protocols that should prevent abuses such as those alleged here. The protocols are designed to ward off attacks on the supply chain modes of production as human rights violations. The utility of the symbolism of these kinds of human rights instruments and institutions is clear; but as noted again in n. 74, the relative ease of complying without changing much is also clear.

73   Jim Yardley and Binyamin Applebaum, "Pope Calls Capitalism a 'Subtle Dictatorship,'" *Toronto Star*, 13 July, 2015, A12.

74   This line of reasoning does not prevent these operators from pretending that they had no idea that their minions were exploiting people mercilessly. When it was reported that Rip Curl, one of Australia's iconic garment-makers, had been using suppliers whose workers were unprotected North Koreans, its chief financial officer told Fairfax Press that "this was a case of a supplier delivering part of their production order to an unauthorised subcontractor, with the production done from an unauthorised factory, in an unauthorised country, without our knowledge or consent, in clear breach of our supplier terms and policies…. [This] company takes its social compliance obligations seriously"; see Nick McKenzie & Richard Barker, "Surf Clothing Label Rip Curl Using 'Slave Labour' to Manufacture Clothes in North Korea," *SMH*, 21 Feb., 2016. This studied ignorance cum innocence kind of declaration is, as we shall see, internalized by policy-makers when establishing the position that entrepreneurs are benign actors whose motives ought not to be questioned.

75   For a spectacular example of how entrepreneurs not only plan but are also in a position to take precautions to avert so-called spills and accidents, note an ongoing controversy about Exxon. The allegations are that, as early as 1979, Exxon's internal researchers were reporting to their employer that fossil fuels were making a major contribution to a potential environmental

disaster. Exxon told no one about these reports, but it did find them credible; see Geoffrey Supran and Naomi Oreskes, "Assessing ExxonMobil's Climate Change Communications (1977–2014)," *Environmental Research Letters*, Vol. 12, no. 8 (IOP Publishing). In the 1980s, internally alerted to the possibility of climate warming, it began to build higher platforms for its offshore drilling to overcome the problem of rising water levels. At the same time, Exxon was contributing to think tanks and lobby groups bolstering the faith of climate change deniers; see Bill McKibben, *TomDispatch*, 19 Feb., 2016; Neela Banerjee, Lisa Song, and David Hasemyer, "Exxon: The Road Not Taken," *Inside Climate News*, 16 Sept., 2015. Now that is planning! This story overlaps with the arguments made below about the way in which regulators are pressured and misled as they look to "virtuous" actors for information and advice on what is practical.

76 World Health Organization, International Program on Chemical Safety—Asbestos, 2004.

77 CTV News, 2 Dec., 2015.

78 The notion that the gouging is criminal in nature is evidenced by the fact that prosecutors have used alleged security law violations in Shkreli's past to put him in the criminal dock; "CEO Is Strutting to Jail," *Fortune*, 5 Aug., 2017. This echoes the way in which Al Capone, suspected of many murders and other vicious crimes, was eventually brought to "justice" by charging him with tax improprieties. His criminality had to be punished even if the formalities of criminal law made it difficult to punish him for his real crimes. That is, we often think of behaviour not caught by the technical rules of law as criminal in nature and, occasionally, find ways of criminally punishing those who betray our norms and values.

79 William D. Cohan, "How Martin Shkreli, the Teen Wolf of Wall Street, Thrived," Opinion Pages, *New York Times*, 18 Dec., 2015. What Martin Shkreli did is par for the course; see Deena Beasly, "Pfizer Hikes US Prices for Over 100 Drugs on January 1," *Reuters*, 10 Jan., 2016; Samantha Allen, "Martin Shkreli Is Just One of Many Pharma A-Holes," *The Daily Beast*, 8 Feb., 2016; Jessie Myerson "Repulsed by Pharma Bro Martin Shkreli? Maybe You Also Hate Capitalism," *In These Times*, 22 Feb., 2016; Fran Quigley, "How Corporations Killed Medicine", *Counterpunch*, 9 Feb., 2016. See also,

"Drug Giant 'Plotted to Destroy Stocks of Cancer Medicines,'" *Daily Mail*, 14 April, 2017, reporting that a South African firm bought five brand cancer medicines from GlaxoSmithKline and then used its legal power to increase prices; it threatened Italian and Spanish government that the needed drugs would be destroyed unless they agreed to price increases. On another front, the story recounted that the National Health Service is investigating how the leukemia drug busulfan went from £5.20 to £65.22 in 2013 in England and Wales and how the blood cancer medicine chlorambucil went from £8.36 per pack to £40.51 per pack. More generally, this drive to control knowledge and to charge for it is a central point of controversy in the battles around trade agreements such as TPPA and TRIPS, n. 65.

80 Lee Fang, "Gun Industry Executives Say Mass Shootings Are Good for Business," *The Intercept*, 3 Dec., 2015.

81 As we characterize those engaged in the illegal drug and armaments trade and in human trafficking, enterprises that are conducted in very much the same way as legalized capitalist profit-maximization enterprises are conducted and for the same reasons: to satisfy wants and not needs; see David Harvey, *The Enigma of Capital and the Crisis of Capitalism* (Oxford: Oxford University Press, 2011), 43: "There are many other ways to amass the social power that money commands: fraud, corruption, banditry, robbery, and illegal trafficking … a serious case can be made that the extra-legal forms are fundamental rather than peripheral to capitalism." In a system where profit is the only calibrator and justification for productive activities, the difference between acceptable and unacceptable behaviour depends only on where law draws the line at any one time, not on a principled criterion such as the obligation to serve human needs first and last. For an extended and enriching argument that the goal of enhancing the qualities of life is not consonant with market capitalism, see John McMurtry, *Unequal Freedoms: The Global Market as an Ethical System* (Toronto: Garamond Press, 1998).

82 Lisa Heinzerling, "Knowing Killing and Environmental Law" (2006), 14 *New York Uni. Environmental L. Jo.* 521.

83 As always, it is important to remember that conduct might also be unethical even if it does not offend existing criminal law, as our notions of what constitutes a crime are far from coherent. Heinzerling is concentrating

on the most obvious coincidences between criminal law and our ethical and moral spheres.

84 For a different reading, one that offers a qualified defence for drawing a line between statistical certainty and particular certainty about a future event, see Kenneth W. Simons, "Statistical Knowledge Deconstructed" (2012), 92 *Boston Uni. L. Rev.*, 1.

85 In a way, Heinzerling mirrors the crime scholarship that, in its search for criteria by which conduct should be criminalized, emphasizes moral turpitude, harm, and a combination of these phenomena—Heinzerling's work, like those strains of scholarship, is pointing to the consequences of a lack of ethics to support her idea that being ethical is worthwhile in practical terms as well as spiritual ones.

86 S. Tombs and D. Whyte, *The Corporate Criminal: Why Corporations Must Be Abolished* (Routledge, 2015), cite a large number of U.K. reports that indicate that up to 30,000 deaths per year could be attributable to air pollution, at 47ff.

87 Tombs and Whyte record that failures to take precautions lead to an inordinate number of cases of food poisoning in the U.K.

88 Per Deane, J., *Janisch v. Coffey* (1984), 155 C.L.R. 549, 579.

89 The law recognizes other special relations that might require a person to act positively to save another person from harm; from T. Weir, *A Casebook on Tort*, 8th ed. (1998): "You need not tell a complete stranger that he is about to fall over a cliff—unless it is your cliff."

90 As quoted by John Kenneth Galbraith, *Age of Uncertainty* (Boston: Houghton Mifflin, 1977), 48.

91 R. Posner, *Economics of Justice* (Cambridge: Harvard University Press, 1981), 83–84.

92 There have been a number of prosecutions, albeit rarely successful, against athletes; for a case that drew a great deal of attention because the violent culture of ice hockey is defended vigorously by many people, see the 2004 prosecution of Todd Bertuzzi, whose attack on a fellow hockey player led to grievous bodily harm. The incident led to anxious questioning as to whether the athlete should be blamed when it was his role to beat up on others to help his team win. It is tempting to draw an analogy to managers

who skirt the law as they chase profits for their employers. Bertuzzi pled guilty and was back playing hockey by the next season; similar cases are recorded by *USLegal*, "Sports Violence," http://sportslaw.uslegal.com/ sports-violence, last consulted on 14 April, 2016. That article concluded by noting that bench-clearing brawls in professional baseball are winked at by law and that "these acts would constitute criminal and civil assaults and batteries but for their occurrence during a sports contest."

93 This notion that it is legally permissible to set up a profit-chasing activity while leaving some hazards and risks in place is well understood and leads to some rather unappealing safety strategies. Thus, Unifor's *Health, Safety & Environment Newsletter*, vol. 3, no. 3, Fall 2015, reported that more and more employers are using Behaviour-Based Safety (BBS) systems that require workers to be educated so that they can do more to minimize the impacts of existing hazards and risks in their workplaces. Ideologically this movement is linked to the belief that, as autonomous individuals, workers agree to risks built into the workplace they have voluntarily decided to join.

94 There is some authority for holding that one may agree to be battered in a barroom fight, at least to the extent that the amount of injury done could be reasonably expected under the circumstances, that is, according to the implicit rules of fairness in such an encounter; see *R. v. Bergner*, (1987), 78 A.R. 331 (Alta. C.A.).

95 For a current example of such supping-with-the-devil bargains, note that in the public debates swirling about the diminution of carbon in our atmosphere, one of the remedies on offer, the trading of poisonous emissions, asks the public to acquiesce to continued harm.

96 E. Tucker, "The Persistence of Market Regulation of Occupational Health and Safety: The Stillbirth of Voluntarism," in G. England, *Essays in Labour Law* (Don Mills, ON: CCH, 1986). He notes that the science that goes into the analyses is not all that determinative as, often, a standard in one jurisdiction is much tougher than it is in others.

97 Keith Ellinson and Van Jones, "Pollution Isn't Colorblind: Environmental Hazards Kill More Black Americans," *Guardian*, 25 July, 2015; Kirsten Lombardi, Talia Burford, and Ronnie Green, "Environmental

Racism Persists. And the EPA Is One Reason Why," The Center for Public
Integrity, 4 Aug., 2015; Charles D. Ellinson, "Racism in the Air You Breathe:
When Where You Live Determines How Fast You Die," The Root, 24 Jan.,
2016; R. Bullard, Dumping in Dixie: Race, Class, and Environmental Quality
(Boulder, CO: Westview Press, 2000). The Bhopal disaster did not occur in
an area where wealthy people live; the pools of toxic waste found in Nova
Scotia are in the black communities' living areas; the mercury in Grassy
Narrows poisoned an Indigenous population; in Australia, the worst incidence of mesothelioma has been found in an Aboriginal settlement in a
place called Wittenoom in Western Australia; the recent publicity given
to the lead pollution of water supplies in Flint, Michigan, revealed that
the adversely affected population was overwhelmingly black; more generally, see the United Church of Christ's 1987 Commission for Racial Justice,
Toxic Waste and Race in the United States: A National Report on the Racial
and Socio-Economic Characteristics of Communities with Hazardous Waste.
In line with the ideas of the plutocrat Rockefeller, corporate capitalism
demands sacrifices, usually by the weak and the vulnerable; see Steve Lerner,
Sacrifice Zones: The Front Lines of Toxic Chemical Exposure in the United
States, 1st ed. (MIT Press, 2010).

98 A. Smith, An Inquiry into the Nature and the Causes of the Wealth of
Nations (New York: Modern Library, 1937), 250. Of course, the deception is
rarely blatant. The corporate sector has learned to employ cadres of highly
credentialled persons to convince governments not to regulate too much,
not to enforce too vigorously.

99 These examples are Canadian ones. All jurisdictions yield similar
examples of dramatic catastrophes that lead to calls for the creation of more
effective criminal sanctions than exist. In Australia, the Esso explosion in
Bass Strait comes to mind; in the U.K., there have been a series of such dis-
asters leading to new legislation; see J. Gobert, "The Politics of Corporate
Manslaughter—The British Experience" (2005), 8 The Flinders Journal of
Law Reform: Special Edition: Industrial Manslaughter, 1. In the U.S. one need
to look no further than the BP disaster in the Gulf of Mexico; in Latvia,
the Riga supermarket collapse was another outrage-raising episode, see
Charles Woolfson and Arunas Juska, "Neo-liberal Austerity and Corporate

Crime: The Collapse of the MAXIMA Supermarket in Riga, Latvia," 2014, *New Solutions*, vol. 24, issue 2, p. 129. The Westray incident is discussed below; for a description of the Lac-Mégantic events, see H. Glasbeek, "Lac-Megantic and the Presumed Innocence of Capitalism," *Class and Capitalism*, 24 July, 2013.

100 I. Ayres and J. Braithwaite, *Responsive Regulation: Transcending the Deregulation Debate* (Oxford University Press, 1992); B. Fisse and J. Braithwaite, *Corporations, Crime and Accountability* (Cambridge: Cambridge University Press, 1993); J. Braithwaite and T. Makkai, "Trust and Compliance," *Policing and Society*, 1994, 1; C. Delitt and B. Fisse, "Civil and Criminal Liability under Australian Securities Regulation: The Possibility of Strategic Enforcement," in C. Delitt and B. Fisse, eds., *Securities Regulation in Australia and New Zealand* (Oxford: Oxford University Press, 1994); F. Haines and A. Sutton, "The Engineer's Dilemma: A Sociological Perspective on Juridification and Regulation" (2003), 39 *Crime, Law and Social Change*, 1; L. Snider, "The Sociology of Corporate Crime: An Obituary," *Theoretical Criminology*, 4, 2, p. 169. This reluctance to classify violations of standards as crimes supports the regulators' obvious inclination to devise penalties that eschew corporal punishment for human operators of violating corporations. This irks the public. There have been many comments about the fact that, despite schemes that robbed millions of people of their savings, hardly any individual has gone to jail. The mantra "too big to fail, too big to jail" has become the common refrain of those many lamentations; see Matt Taibbi, *The Divide: American Injustice in the Age of the Wealth Gap* (Melbourne/London: Scribe, 2014); Charles H. Ferguson, *Predator Nation: Corporate Criminals, Political Corruption and the Hijacking of America* (Crown Publishing Group, 2012) (a follow-up on his film *Inside Job*). For recent headlines that typify the malaise all but the policy-makers and regulators feel, see David Kravets, "Manslaughter Charges Dropped in BP Spill Case—Nobody from BP Will Go to Prison," *ArsTechnica*, 3 Dec., 2015; Robert H. Tillman and Henry Pontell, "Corporate Fraud Demands Criminal Time," Opinion Pages, *New York Times*, 29 June, 2016.

101 Steve Tombs, "Crisis, What Crisis? Regulation and the Academic Orthodoxy" (2015) 54 *The Howard Jo. of Criminal Justice* 57, provides a most

useful overview of this literature and a persuasive and trenchant criticism of its output in the wake of the great financial crisis.

102 Steve Tombs, "Crisis, What Crisis?...," 67.

103 F. Pearce and S. Tombs, *Toxic Capitalism: Corporate Crimes and the Chemical Industry* (Toronto: Canadian Scholars Press, 1998); see also S. Box, *Corporate Crime* (Essex: Pearson Education, 1999); S. Bittle, *Still Dying for a Living: Corporate Criminality after the Westray Mine Disaster* (UBC Press, 2012); Tombs and Whyte, *The Corporate Criminal*; Friedrich Engels, *The Condition of the English Working Class*, Panther Edition (1969); Glasbeek, *Wealth by Stealth*.

104 Nova Scotia, *Report of the Westray Mine Public Inquiry: A Predictable Path to Disaster* (Richards, 1997).

105 For a thorough account of the felt need to reform the law and the instinctive reluctance to do so, see Bittle, *Still Dying for a Living*.

106 Glasbeek, "Missing the Targets—Bill C-45: Reforming the Status Quo to Maintain the Status Quo" (2013) 11 *Policy and Practice in Health and Safety* 9; Bittle, *Still Dying for a Living*; S. Tombs and D. Whyte, "A Deadly Consensus: Worker Safety and Regulatory Degradation under New Labour" (2010), 50 *Br. Jo. Of Criminology*, 46; *The Flinders Journal of Law Reform*, Special Edition—Industrial Manslaughter (2005), vol. 8, issue 1.

107 Norm Keith, "After 10 Years, Bill C-45 Yields Few Prosecutions," *Occupational Safety*, www.cos-mag.com, 23 April, 2014; in Australia, there has not yet been a prosecution under the new Commonwealth corporate crime-creating provisions.

108 D. Harvey, *The Enigma of Capital and the Crisis of Capitalism* (Oxford: Oxford University Press, 2010); D. Korten, "From Buccaneers to Profiteers: On the Origin of Corporations," *YES! Magazine*, 8 March, 2011, n. 61.

109 William Dalrymple, "The East India Company: The Original Corporate Raiders," *The Guardian*, 4 March, 2015.

110 Edward E. Baptist, *The Half Has Never Been Told: Slavery and the Making of American Capitalism* (Basic Books, 2014).

111 D. Hay and P. Craven, eds., *Masters, Servants and Magistrates in Britain and the Empire, 1562–1955* (University of North Carolina Press, 2004).

112 Lee Drutman, "How Corporate Lobbyists Conquered American Democracy," *The Atlantic*, 20 April, 2016.

113 Lee Fang, "Former Tax Lobbyists Are Writing the Rules on Tax Dodging," *The Intercept*, 27 April, 2016.

114 Seamus Milne, "Corporate Power Has Turned Britain into a Corrupt State," *The Guardian*, 5 June, 2013; the insidious ways in which this massaging might work is glimpsed from a CBC news item: "CRA Executives Treated to Soirees at Private Club amid KPMG Probe," *CBC News* posted 17 April, 2016.

115 Arundhati Roy, "The Doctor and the Saint," introduction to B.R. Ambedkar, *Annihilation of Caste*, ed. S. Anad (New Dehli: Navayana Publishing, 2014), 27; see also Tombs and Whyte, *The Corporate Criminal*, citing Coghlan and Mackenzie, "Revealed—The Capitalist Network That Runs the World," *New Scientist*, No. 2835, 2011, which reports that there were 37 million companies in the world and that 1,348 of interlocked companies shared 20% of global operating revenues and that, within this network, 147 corporations owned 40% of its wealth; the authors also use Weismann, "Corporate Power Since 1980," *Common Dreams*, 1 June, 2007, for the finding that the markets in a variety of industries, such as oil, food, finance, pharmaceuticals, tobacco, aircraft, defence contracting, utilities, energy, insurance, hotels, mining, and media were oligopolistic, that is, concentrated, non-competitive markets.

116 The many codes of conduct that have been designed to push corporate actors to acknowledge the needs of stakeholders other than shareholders urge that corporations abide by existing laws and act in a socially responsible manner. Corporations are asked to adopt such codes and then to live by them. But for the most part (different approaches are becoming visible in India and, to some extent, China), in order to get adoption, the codes are intended not to be legally enforceable, to be voluntary; see J.J. Du Plessis, A. Hargovan, A. Bagaric, and J. Harris, *Principles of Contemporary Corporate Governance*, 3rd ed. (Cambridge University Press, 2015). Efforts are made to put pressure on adopting corporations by having them report on how they implement their voluntary undertakings. This is to be contrasted with the legislated and enforceable corporate governance rules that have followed each and every

one of the many financial crises over the last three decades. They are designed to safeguard corporate actors and investors and lead to positive legal duties. Inasmuch as voluntary codes of conduct ask corporations to think about the environment and society at large, they may have a marginal impact.

117 E. Hobsbawm, *The Age of Extremes: A History of the World, 1914–1991* (New York: Vintage, 1996).

118 John Paluszek, *Will the Corporation Survive?* (Reston, VA: Reston Publishing Company, 1977).

119 David Vogel, *National Styles of Regulation: Environmental Policy in Great Britain and the United States* (Ithaca, NY: Cornell University Press, 1986).

120 See Herbert Docena, "To Change the Heart and Soul: How Elites Contained the Climate Justice Movement," *The Bullet*, Socialist Project, E-Bulletin No. 1210, 22 Jan., 2016.

121 See E. Mason, ed., *The Corporation in Modern Society* (Atheneum, 1966).

122 Jane Anne Morris, "Corporate Social Responsibility: Kick the Habit," *By What Authority?: Program on Corporations, Law & Democracy (POCLAD)*, vol. 2, no. 2, Spring 2000.

123 John Lorinc, "The Root of All Evil: Like It or Not, You Are Investing in Sin Stocks," *The Walrus*, Jan./Feb. 2016.

124 Daniel Bell, *The End of Ideology: The Exhaustion of Political Ideas in the Fifties* (New York: Free Press, 1965).

125 Michel J. Crozier, Samuel P. Huntington, and Joji Watanuki, *The Crisis of Democracy: Report of the Governability of Democracies to the Trilateral Commission* (NYU Press, 1975).

126 Refer to Paul Smith, Eric Tucker, and Work Choices comment in n. 60.

127 Stanley Deetz, *Democracy in an Age of Corporate Colonization* (SUNY Press, 1992).

128 Francis Fukuyama, *The End of History and the Last Man* (Simon & Shuster, 2006; first pub. 1992).

129 Another way to look at the gap between our legal expectations and the treatment of corporations and their controllers and beneficiaries

is provided by Joshua Barkan's *Corporate Sovereignty: Law and Government under Capitalism* (Minneapolis/London: University of Minneapolis Press, 2013). He argues that to see corporations (as conventional wisdom does) through a lens that distinguishes between the economic and political spheres leads corporations to be viewed as an economic tool. Relying on the work of Giorgio Agamben, *Homo Sacer: Sovereign Power and Real Life* (Stanford: Stanford University Press, 1998), Barkan argues that this approach is bound to fail because it misunderstands the position occupied by the corporation in our political economy. In his view, it is not just an economic entity created by the state to allow individuals to pursue their own and, thereby, state purposes. While they are created by law, giving corporations the appearance of being totally subject to the state and its law, they are intended to be constituent parts of another sphere, one sovereign in its own right. Relying on Agamben's concept that law defines itself by what it excludes, Barkan argues that the corporation is created as the other, as belonging to the ban (to use Agamben's descriptor). The extent of the exclusion establishes the corporations' sphere of sovereign operation and existence. To this extent, a corporation acts as an alternate sovereign domain, sometimes in opposition, to the very state law that established it. There is, in Barkan's language, a doubling of sovereignty, state law being, in some measure, inapplicable to the corporation as a "banned" sovereign. Barkan's book documents the historical manifestations of this characterization of corporations to buttress his contention that there is a doubling of sovereignty. To justify a state creature to be beyond the state's reach, even when on occasions its conduct leads to tension-creating and flat-out oppositional behaviours, the state and corporate sovereigns must be able to argue effectively that this inapplicability of law and its standards leads to the public good. It is an empirical claim to legitimate a political economic regime that does not sit well with accepted dogma. From the vantage point of this essay, this would signify that liberal law is not so much distorted to assist corporate capitalism as it is inapposite to govern its behaviour. If this is not seen or accepted, it is inevitable that attempts will be made to subject corporations to principles and rules that clash with the reality of that separate sovereignty. This is an exciting thesis, one with the potential to enrich the work of critical scholars. It deserves more attention than can be given it here. I will restrict myself to claim that there is some congruence between this work and Barkan's thesis. Like Barkan, this paper also is intent on raising questions about the ideological constraints that bound our ability to deal with the problem of the corporate institution in Anglo-American jurisdictions. As Barkan puts it, his aim is "to expose us to the invisible, unrecognized, and repressed logics that govern our understanding of corporate power" (p. 18), to create an opening that what is may be challenged and changed. I share the goal.

130 David Korten, "Why the Economy Should Stop Growing—and Just Grow Up," *YES! Magazine*, 6 May, 2016. For more details of this argument, see my *Class Privilege*; see also Herman Daly, "Dear Paul Krugman: Is GDP Growth Making Us Richer or Poorer?," *The Daly News*, 10 May, 2014; Kent Greenfield, "New Principles for Corporate Law" (2005), *Hastings Bus. L. Jo.* 87; Elinor Ostrom, *Governing the Commons: The Evolution of Institutions for Collective Action*, reissue ed. (Cambridge University Press, 2015).

131 As quoted in M. Albert, *Moving Forward: Programme for a Participatory Democracy* (AK Press, 2001), 128.

132 Tombs and Whyte, *The Corporate Criminal*. This concentrates on the harms done by corporate actors and on our existing institutions' relative impotence. This impotence is attributed to our internalization of TINA. The book highlights the lack of benefits derived from generating wealth by means of the tool specially designed to serve the capitalist project rather than a more humanistic and humane one.

133 The hold this notion that capital should be trusted in order to enhance its willingness to invest has on our public policy-makers is on display in a bill proposed in Australia. Industry would be allowed to self-assess whether a chemical new to Australia was low-risk and should be brought to market without telling any regulatory body about this; see Nicole Hasham, "Industrial Chemicals: Turnbull Government Moves to Slash Safety Testing Regulations," *WAToday*, 20 Aug., 2017. This approach differs sharply from that of those who, like me, want to hold those who control, and benefit from, corporate behaviour responsible for the corporation's initiatives; see Frank Partnoy, "Corporations and Human Life" (2017), *40 Seattle Uni. Law Rev.*, 399.

134 Harry Glasbeek, "The James Hardie Directors: A Case of Missing Directors and Misdirections by Law" (2013), 28 *Aust. J. Corp. Law*, 107; "Piercing on Steroids" (2014), 29 *Aust. J. Corp. Law*, 233; *Class Privilege*, 124.

135 Ramsay and Blair, "Ownership Concentration, Institutional Investment and Corporate Governance" (1993); G.P. Stapledon, "The Structure of Share Ownership and Control: The Potential for Institutional Investor Activism" (1995), 18 *U.N.S.W. L. Jo.* 250; Lampda and Stapledon, "Public Law & Legal Theory Working Paper No. 20" (Faculty of Law, University of Melbourne, 2001).

136 Morck, Strangeland, and Yeung; "Inherited Wealth, Corporate Control & Economic Growth: The Canadian Disease?" in Morck, ed., *Concentrated Corporate Ownership* (National Bureau of Economic Research, 2000); Rao and Lee-Sing, "Governance Structure: Corporate Decision-Making and Firm Performance," Working Paper 7, Industry Canada, March 1996. Note that, where corporations are private ones, the owners/controllers are easier to spot and that, when corporations are small and not traded at all (a sector that constitutes the majority of corporate actors), the identity of those on whose behalf the corporation is required to act and by whom they are told to do so is totally un-mysterious. It is also noteworthy that, even in the U.S., there is a good deal of evidence that many publicly traded corporations are closely controlled by a few people; Harold Demetz, "The Structure of Ownership of the Firm" (1983), 26 *Jo. L.& Eco.* 388; Harold Demetz and Belen Villalonga, "Ownership Structure and Corporate Performance" (2001), 7 *Journal of Corporate Finance*, 209, which finds that the five largest shareholders in a large sample of U.S. firms hold 20% to 60% of the voting shares; see also Clifford G. Holderness, "The Myth of Diffuse Ownership in the United States" (2009), 22 *The Review of Financial Studies* 1377; Nina Mendelson, "A Controlled Approach to Shareholder Liability for Corporate Torts" (2002), 102 *Col L. Jo.* 1203.

137 La Porta et al., "Corporate Ownership around the World" (1999), 54 *Jo. of Fin.* 471.

138 Bertrand Russell, "Freedom in Society," *Harper's Magazine*, April 1926.